A SAVAGE REPUBLIC

INSIDE THE PLOT TO DESTROY AMERICA

MICHAEL SAVAGE

BOMBARDIER
BOOKS

Published by Bombardier Books
An Imprint of Post Hill Press
ISBN: 979-8-88845-382-7
ISBN (eBook): 979-8-88845-383-4

A Savage Republic:
Inside the Plot to Destroy America
© 2023 by Michael Savage
All Rights Reserved

Post Hill Press
New York • Nashville
posthillpress.com

Published in the United States of America
1 2 3 4 5 6 7 8 9 10

*Dedicated to all the military heroes
who sacrificed for our freedoms.*

CONTENTS

PREFACE

————

IT'S BEEN SAID THAT those who have knowledge don't predict. Predicting the future is very complicated based upon so many diverse outcomes. Those who have the power to shape the future can better predict the future than I. However, I recently asked my followers on social media, "What are your predictions about the world and the United States?" Here are some of their replies:

Will NATO consider Russia weak enough to put boots on the ground? Will Biden be replaced? Will Joe Manchin or Gavin Newsom run for president? Will the U.S. economy continue its decline? Will there be a U.S. currency crisis resulting in a world digital currency? Will there be a continued push to draw us into war with Russia? Will Taiwan be attacked? Will there be food shortages? Will Iran go nuclear? Will there be another pandemic? Will there be more revelations about UFOs? Will eating turkeys be outlawed and we'll be forced to eat insects? Will Biden outlaw Thanksgiving?

Now, here are some funny ones:

Will Kamala bring word salad to Thanksgiving dinner?

Thanksgiving? Oh, that's when Joe Biden will wish us a Happy Fourth of July, 2023!

Jesus will come back to Earth to save mankind. Unfortunately, the Democrats will imprison him forever because he appeared to be standing on a BLM mural painted on the road. Afterwards there is a gay-trans orgy on the mural to honor it, and the imprisonment of Jesus the bigot.

Can anyone really predict what might happen in this nation and the world by the end of this year? With a totally corrupt government and a complicit media virtually anything is possible.

CHAPTER 1

THE CIVIL WAR IS HERE

———

We're not going to see massive armies of Americans
marching toward each other. It's a war of ideas.
Americans are roughly split into three political groups:
conservative, libertarian, and progressive. And it is this
last group that has declared war against the other two.

———

I N 2013, I WROTE a book titled, *Stop the Coming Civil War*. I said that this nation was in real trouble and that the seeds of a second conflagration had been sown. Ten years later, it's not the *coming* civil war. We're in it. It's being run by the far left.

I predicted in 2013 and I predict now that the war will not be between the states but between true patriots who believe in our nation's founding principles and those whom I believe are working every day to undermine those principles and change the very nature of our country. I said in that 2013 book that people like Biden and Harris and the shadowy people behind them are transforming America in front of our eyes. I said then that it won't be a war of bullets and blood but one of commitment to freedom and the courage of conviction.

We're facing more than just political differences now. The split between the right and the left is irreparable. I've been raising my voice for more than 25 years, and I'm telling you that the situation is urgent. We're in the red zone. Today I'm raising my voice again even louder because the civil war is upon us.

Apparently, the left didn't hear me because they want a civil war. I'm trying to galvanize every liberty-loving American and warn the enemies of our way of life that the time has come. The line must be drawn.

It is our way of life the left wants to destroy. President Biden tells you that he wants to "build back better," a slogan he was spoon fed by the World Economic Forum, headed by the communist Klaus Schwab. Well, just think for a moment what those words mean. You can only *build back* something that has been torn down. This is the plot the globalists have conceived: They want to tear down Western civilization, most importantly its crown jewel, the United States, and "build it back" into something alien to our principles and under their complete control.

Once you understand this plot against our way of life, you can see it being executed everywhere. Why have so many of our top military commanders been pushed aside by Biden after years of brave service? Why is our foreign policy establishment reaching out to Iran, which is now racing to develop nuclear weapons?

Russia invaded Ukraine as a direct result of the anti-Russian rhetoric and actions of Obama, Clinton, Lindsay Graham, and more recently Biden and his team of fanatics. They are now pitting the Israelis against Arabs again in the Middle East after Trump had brought peace. How does this secure our freedom and our way of life?

Negligent immigration law enforcement under this administration allows millions of illegal aliens to pour over the southern border not only with little fear of penalty but rather welcomed in by the profiteers in so many so-called religious groups like Catholic Charities. The civil war is here, and the border is one of its many battlefields.

How do we save the nation? How do we end the civil war that has finally come? How do we preserve the middle class? How do we stop the war that has been going on against our borders, language, and culture? How do we stop the war on our military? How do we stop the war on the middle class? How do we stop the war in

American medicine, namely COVID? How do we stop Biden's war on civil rights? How do we stop Fauci's war on science? How do we stop Biden's attack on our schools?

THE BIDEN BAIT AND SWITCH

In April 2021, I saw an article that was so deceptive about Nancy Pelosi and packing the Supreme Court that I think it's worth revisiting. And of all places, it was in Murdoch's *New York Post* and was titled, "Pelosi Rejects Fellow Democrats' 'Court-Packing' Bill, Will Not Bring It to Vote."[1] When I read the headline, I thought, "Wow, that's great. She's a centrist." But it was a lie. When you read the article carefully, you find that Pelosi actually said, "I don't know that that's a good idea or bad idea. I think it's an idea that ought to be considered. And I think the president's taking the right approach too, to have a commission to study such a thing. It's a big step."

Pelosi goes on to say that packing the Court is "not out of the question" and that it has been "done before" in the history of our country—a long time ago.

So the article's headline and opening comments made Pelosi look reasonable, while the substance of her comments is that she actually supports packing the Court. This is a recurring theme not only since Biden was inaugurated but also throughout his absentee campaign. The Democrats and the media keep selling us centrism and delivering radical leftist policies that even many Democrats didn't vote for.

The Democrats pulled the same bait and switch on infrastructure. There was broad bipartisan consensus on passing appropriations for what has always been considered "infrastructure." I'm talking about roads, bridges, airports, bus stations—the basic foundation of a commercial society. But that's not what Biden tried to ram through as infrastructure.

Calling it "Build Back Better," a name lifted from the communist World Economic Forum, Biden's phony infrastructure package was actually a $3.5 trillion bonanza of massive new welfare spending combined with elements of the insane Green New Deal promoted by "Occasional Cortex" (aka Alexandria Ocasio-Cortez) and other extremist socialists.[2]

It included up to $20,000 in handouts to low-income first-time homebuyers. It would provide $14,000 to homeowners and the contractors they'd hire to make their homes more energy efficient. Of course, the contractors would have to be union shops. The union contractors would also get a $200 bonus for every customer from a "community of racial or minority ethnic concentration."

This isn't infrastructure; it's social engineering. And it's just another example of the Biden administration putting on the guise of centrist moderation while pushing the kind of radical leftist policy you'd expect from the worst of the candidates Democratic voters rejected in the 2020 primaries.

Until Republicans are back in control, nobody will stop them other than the two Democratic senators who will not be pressured to go along with the madness of our times.

THE LEFTIST INSURGENCY

This is the nature of the civil war in which we find ourselves in. We're not going to see massive armies of Americans marching toward each other. It's a war of ideas. Americans are roughly split into three political groups: conservative, libertarian, and so-called progressives. And it is this last group that has declared war against the other two.

What's a libertarian? What's a liberal? What's a conservative? When libertarians drive a truck in a protest, it's a peaceful protest.

They want government off their backs. No vaccine mandates. That's the issue today.

Now we contrast that with a modern liberal or progressive today driving a truck. The liberal says, "Not only will I protest what I'm going to protest, but I'm going to crash my truck into a Nordstrom and steal the jewelry and clothing. That's what the pickup bed is for."

This is what liberalism has become because it's been taken over by anarchists, radical progressives, and Black Lives Matter. There are no classical liberals anymore as far as I can tell. They've all become activists and rather violent and coercive.

So let's look at the origins of this without getting into a whole lecture on it. What is it all about? Ronald Reagan explained it best. It's very simple: less government. Get out of my pocket, get off my back, and let me have more control over my own destiny. This really makes sense. This is what libertarianism is.

Basically, classical liberalism was very similar. It was a breakaway from powerful governments backed by state churches and monarchies, and it focused on freedom of the individual. That was the original liberalism. But look at what it's become today—so-called progressivism. It's become violent and coercive. You've got entertainers who used to be libertarians. Many have become coercive, saying that people who don't take vaccines should be turned away from hospitals and sent home to die.[3] How do people transform into these characters who are the opposite of what they began as?

That leaves conservatives. What is it to be conservative? Many of us who are on the right are really a mixture of libertarian and conservative. We want limited government, but we don't believe in anarchy. This is where libertarianism gets lost. When people start saying no government, that's crazy!

We have lost the liberals because they no longer even think of themselves as progressives. They've moved to radical socialism. And for them, it is their ideology to the exclusion of anyone else's ideology. You must accept what they believe or you are "a deplorable" or un-American. And that is how they have forced their agenda on us.

They've emerged from rebelling against churches and monarchies and overtly powerful governments to becoming an overly powerful, coercive force unto themselves. And where this goes is very dangerous. Progressivism is leading to National Socialism. Need I remind anyone reading this what National Socialism is?

National Socialism was Nazism. That's what Hitler introduced into Germany—National Socialism—and we're not too far away from that here in America today. When you listen to Occasional Cortex, she sounds like a National Socialist. Pelosi is a fascist or a National Socialist. The Nazis made you salute and praise the Führer; the Democrats make you say the pronouns. Democrats conducted show trials for the supposed January 6 insurrectionists and constructed an American Gestapo to hunt down more. These are very dangerous times.

STALINIST BIDEN

There are also parallels to another of the twentieth-century totalitarian regimes, the Soviet Union. People must learn history in order not to repeat it. I'm going to talk about the man who I think New York prosecutor Alvin Bragg is copying in terms of his handling of his "case" against former President Donald Trump. But I'll start by asking this: Why did it take so long to put the crypto crook Sam Bankman-Fried behind bars? After all, he allegedly pulled off the largest financial scam in American history and then was released on minimal bail to live in his parents' mansion in Palo Alto. This is American justice under the Biden Stalinist regime.

On the one hand, they let violent criminals out of jail to rape and murder again and allow financial criminals like Bankman-Fried to live in luxury, while, on the other hand, they pursue trumped-up (no pun intended) or plain fabricated crimes against innocent conservatives. They've even gone after a former president of the United States over what looks like, at most, a bookkeeping error. This after finally obtaining President Trump's tax returns after all these years. Notice that he isn't being charged with tax evasion. Why not? Is it because they want to take it easy on him? Or is it because *he never evaded taxes?*

It's very important that people understand who Donald Trump is in order to know Bragg's prosecution is a miscarriage of justice. We know that it's the weaponization of the legal system and un-American at its core. But who is the man, Donald Trump?

We saw him on the night before he was indicted at his Florida golf club. Everything was perfect that night. My family was amazed at how his club is managed down to the nth degree. This is how the man runs his life. At the same time, we looked at him and thought he would be crushed by this impending doom hanging over his head. If it was bothering him, he didn't show it. He has to be the strongest guy I ever met.

The former president went on to give a speech to an audience of about three hundred people in the dining room. You would have thought he would talk about his travails, his legal trouble. Instead, he talked about golf and the golf club. I was truly amazed that he could do that under such pressure.

I told President Trump that I had been waiting to see him to tell him one thing: that Alvin Bragg is emulating the man who conducted Josef Stalin's reign of terror. I was talking about Lavrentiy Beria, the sadistic mass murderer. He is the one who said, "Show me the man, and I'll show you the crime." He was proud that he could prove criminal conduct on anyone, even the innocent.

Now, you well know, we all know, that under the United States Constitution there is a presumption of innocence that emanates from the Fifth, Sixth, and Fourteenth Amendments. In many legal trials in the Soviet Union, it was precisely the opposite. There was a presumption of guilt. If we let the criminal Biden regime twist America and America's laws and jurisprudence into something like the Soviet system, none of us will be safe.

The Biden regime's stooge, New York District Attorney Alvin Bragg, is following this Soviet model. He certainly isn't following the U.S. Constitution's model. It's a nightmare. And again, we have to remember the main point about this case. Hush payments may be sleazy, but they are not illegal. This is why Bragg is stretching the law to say that although the hush payment was legal, the way it was reported was illegal. It's a bookkeeping error that they're trying to exaggerate into a tax crime, as if President Trump were Al Capone. It's ridiculous.

Again, let's not forget that the Democrats pursued President Trump's tax records for more than six years. They used every dirty trick and corrupt legal maneuver to get them—and *this is all they have*. They can't manufacture a more serious charge because the man is innocent. As attorney and judge Sol Wachtler famously said, a grand jury will indict a ham sandwich.

There is a silver lining to this dark cloud of injustice. People who were lukewarm to Donald Trump before began rallying behind him once these latest witch hunts began. Many of the people saying that he'd had his time are all behind him now. People previously ambivalent about Trump are so angry and so motivated that it appears the Democrats, as smart and as clever as they think they are, have made the greatest blunder of their lives.

This is not only the case for Trump supporters but also for many decent liberals. There are many in America who are still classical liberals. They're not all bad. We must remember that a bird needs two wings to fly. When you break off one wing, the bird flies in circles. And that's what the left has been doing to this country, trying to break the right wing off the bird called America. As a result, the American eagle is crashing to earth.

America is awakening to the Biden criminal regime. This is why I believe Donald Trump is going to weather this storm no matter what they do to him. If they come and arrest him, he'll run for office from prison—and win.

I've seen a slight change even among establishment Republicans moving over to Trump's side because of this case. Rich Lowry of the *National Review*, for example, was no fan of Donald Trump. Now he writes that Bragg will cross the Rubicon and divide the nation by indicting Trump.[4] Attorney Jonathan Turley compared Bragg to Frankenstein, saying he brought a criminal case back from the dead, constructed out of parts from both state and federal codes. He calls it "the ultimate gravedigger charge" but also says it may have reanimated Trump's chances.[5]

So, people who are very anti-Trump or just not really for Trump are understanding what's at stake here. The Democrats made a huge mistake here. The aforementioned Beria, who tortured people to death in slave labor camps, infamously said, "Show me the man, and I'll show you the crime." He targeted the man first and then proceeded to find or fabricate a crime. It's chilling to realize that this is what the Biden crime family is now doing to so many people. It is not only Donald Trump but all those military veterans who may have rioted on that infamous January 6 now rotting in stinking prisons in Washington, DC, most of whom committed no crimes whatsoever.

THE NEW *KULAKS*

In Soviet Russia, the Bolshevik Revolution started with a hatred toward farmers. What we're seeing here is a hatred against white people stirred by the president himself. This is an insurgency of sustained and distributed conflict, with violence being carried out by the left. Consider how the CIA defines insurgency in its *Guide to the Analysis of Insurgency*:

> A conflict in the preinsurgency stage is difficult to detect because most activities are underground, and the insurgency has yet to make its presence felt through the use of violence. Moreover, actions conducted in the open can easily be dismissed as nonviolent political activity. During this stage, an insurgent movement is beginning to organize: leadership is emerging, and the insurgents are establishing a grievance and a group identity, beginning to recruit and train members, and stockpiling arms and supplies.[6]

This is exactly where we are. But this has happened in other places in the world as well. Many civil wars in the world did not and do not have soldiers marching on the battlefield. Did you know that in the early stage of the Syrian civil war, it was fought by paramilitary groups fighting in neighborhoods? It was the same for 30 years in Ireland? Groups of insurgents policed the streets. They "disappeared" people from their homes. They kidnapped and removed them. They assassinated political enemies and bombed buildings.

There was a so-called Colombian conflict, which was really a civil war. It was an asymmetrical war that lasted almost 60 years with guerrilla groups fighting each other and the government—most famously the Revolutionary Armed Forces of Colombia, the

People's Army (FARC-EP and FARC). You may have seen them in "narco shows." There were also right-wing groups that colluded with the police and assassinated leftist political leaders.

This is what the type of civil war I'm talking about looks like. It is armed groups with various objectives trying to take over territory with great cultural and political influence. And they're often violent. If America continues to go down the road of civil war, it's not going to look like it did in 1860. It will look more like Belfast in 1972 or Aleppo in 2011.

There are important differences. The United States is a very big country. It's not a small country like Ireland. Social media are clearly fueling the conflict. Our population is heavily armed. Everyone's frightened. I don't care who you are. Everybody knows that something is wrong.

I never thought I'd see apartheid in America, but that is what we have. White people are excluded from graduations, called every name under the sun, and taught to hate their own race. How is this even possible?

I mentioned Stalin's Russia because there is another historical precedent for this. It wasn't about race under Stalin; it was about class warfare. Before the farms were taken over by the state, which then mismanaged them so badly that 30 million Russians died in a famine, there was first a hatred projected against farmers.

Stalin attacked the farmers first by slandering them, giving them the name *kulak*. *Kulak* has a few different meanings in Russian: "exploiter," "opportunist," etc. The *kulaks* were demonized as anticommunist and greedy for owning too many acres of land and being modestly affluent. They became scapegoats for the failure of communism on the reasoning that the wealth they created was somehow stolen from their comrades.

This is exactly what's going on in America today toward white people. This is coming from President Biden, social media, the universities, from blacks and white communists. They're targeting white people the way the farmers were targeted in Russia. Their relative success is characterized as resulting from their oppression of people of other races. It makes no more sense than did demonization of the *kulaks*, but the demagogues don't appeal to reason. They tap into the worst of people's emotions: envy.

The farmers were first called kulaks, and then something horrible happened: Stalin sent his police in to steal their grain. He said that they were hoarding it for profit, "profiteering." And not only did these violent police steal the grain from poor farmers living in huts, but they also boasted that they even stole their shoes and the pillows from underneath their sleeping children's heads.[7]

Then the brutality started. Stalin recruited street thugs—Marxist street thugs from the cities. Sound familiar? Sound like Black Lives Matter? Or perhaps Antifa? Stalin sent those violent street thugs out to the farms to beat and kill the farmers. It starts with hate, and then the atrocities follow—and the ones doing the killing and the hating justify it. They justify their violence as being defensive because the targeted group is oppressing them or even just racist.

Do you understand what's going on now? Couple this with social media that are not controlling this from the left and you'll have to say that we're already in a state of civil war.

If you look at Syria, Iraq, Ukraine, and Ireland, it is clear that the modern American equivalent is happening here. Has the collapse occurred? No, not yet. Many of you can put it out of your minds by watching movies on Netflix or stuffing your face with garbage from McDonald's. But I am telling you that things could accelerate quickly from here. It all could collapse.

If you want to stop Joe Biden and the so-called woke culture from turning us into slaves and turning this reality into another world that you can never escape, you have to wake up to the fact that the civil war has begun, and you must either stand up or kneel down. There is no third choice.

THE REAL ARMED INSURRECTION

Let's look at Portland, Oregon. There's a study examining what's going on in Portland. And a man named Robert Evans, who's been living in Portland and covering the activities there ever since they began, said this: "I think it's preparing everyone for the big one. At some point, if this continues, you will have three large groups of armed people show up and begin firing at each other with live rounds and you'll have multiple casualties. Those three groups are, broadly, the left, the right, and law enforcement."[8]

Has it happened yet? No, but we are very close. Just add reprisals and shootings, and we will be Syria. Evans said that Syria wasn't just the army versus the people. It was Assad *and* his paramilitaries. And so, we could wind up like Syria. The number of weapons in this country is greater than the number available in Syria at the time. We've got more than 100 million weapons in private hands. We've had a spike of about eight million weapons purchased in the last year, leading to a nationwide ammo shortage.[9] What do you think is going on with more than 100 million weapons in people's hands and a spike in weapon purchases, especially since Biden's gang took over?

Now we've had spikes in firearm sales in the past. They usually happen after a mass shooting when people buy weapons in a panic, believing that guns are going to be made illegal. The spikes have gotten much bigger now. Almost four million guns were sold in America in March of 2020.[10] In June of 2021, the FBI conducted

3.9 million background checks for guns, and in January 2021, 4.3 million checks were conducted, compared with just 2.7 million in January 2020. Arms manufacturers cannot make ammunition fast enough to keep up with the demand. Moreover, body armor sales are up by as much as 600 percent for some manufacturers.[11]

Biden is not helping. The left-wing paramilitary groups that already exist are clashing with police over every reason imaginable. If a criminal is shot dead in the street as he flees the police, whether it's by accident or on purpose, they start to burn and loot. Meanwhile, the politicians look the other way. Biden says nothing. This is very similar to what's gone on in other countries.

We're in a polarized society in which the extreme left is very powerful and may succeed. If they do, society will fundamentally change, and we need to be fearful of that.

In *The Strategy of Tension: Understanding State Labeling Processes and Double-Binds*, Matt Clement and Vincenzo Scalia talk about how the Italian state exploited fear and paranoia to maintain power. Sound familiar? It starts a cycle that goes from repression of dissent to isolation of the repressed groups to terrorism.

So, in this climate of polarization and paranoia, many of us don't know what the truth is. And many of us just turn away and say, "I don't care whose fault it is. I just don't want it to happen." You want it to go away, and you think it's going to go away, but it won't go away. The communists are on the rise. Those on the right who stood up were labeled Nazis, Ku Klux Klan, and white supremacists, but those on the left are called protesters. Where is the truth? No one cares what the truth is. All they do is turn their heads away, and they want it to end. It won't end!

And so people turn inward. They do other things. The political machinery of America is broken. Nobody has confidence in the government—absolutely no confidence in Joe Biden, no confidence in Kamala Harris, and no confidence in either party. They simply hate.

So, we're now at the point where this could explode even further. And there are many parallels between Italy at that time and America now, and much depends on what comes next. Trump lost. You thought that might have defused the left somewhat. Oh, he's gone. We're going to have just a wonderful time now. But that didn't happen.

The social media czarinas are letting the extremists on both sides run wild but mainly killing off those on the right and letting those on the left spew hatred via their platforms. You wonder if somebody is going to step in. How can we stop this?

The reality is that tens of millions of people are armed to the teeth. Some of them are prepared to murder their countrymen. Some are actually looking forward to it. Is Joe Biden helping or hurting? We have a civil war right now that is not yet a hot war, but I am telling you as I sit here that what I predicted in my earlier books is happening now.

Biden is Obama's puppet; the third Obama term is underway. All you have to do is look at what's going on in America: the hatred of the police and a new deal with Iran (which was speeding along with its centrifuges to make atomic weapons). There is a quote by Thomas Corwin to Abraham Lincoln in 1861 that I put in my book years ago. Corwin said: "I cannot comprehend the madness of the times. Treason is in the air around us everywhere—it goes by the name of patriotism."

A POST-CONSTITUTIONAL SOCIETY

I fear the worst because right now, as you know, Americans are angrier and more divided than I've seen them since the 1960s. And what fires this rage is that we have become a post-constitutional society. The system has been turned upside down. What's right is wrong. What's good is bad. What's subversive is patriotic. We now exist at the whim of the social media magnates and the lobbyists who control a government that is likely to do anything it wants to satisfy its lust for power.

At this moment, the nation is a tinderbox that can easily go up in flames. You can see it happening already in Minneapolis. Why when a black man killed a grandfather and his wife and their two grandchildren, all white, and then killed two air-conditioning men on the property were there no riots?[12] Because when the left or a member of one of their protected groups does it, it's okay.

America is a tinderbox that could easily go up in flames because there's going to be a point at which nobody can take this anymore. We are increasingly under the thumb of an administration that is destroying our 200-year-old tradition of defending our borders, language, and culture and replacing it with a culture of statelessness and corruption. Any American who stands up against this tyranny, good, God-fearing people who have had enough of seeing their civil rights trampled, their jobs vanish, their income seized through taxation, the border being overrun, their children poisoned with LGBTQ+ propaganda, is now targeted as an enemy of the state.

People don't know what to do, but right now we're in a place that mirrors the darkest days of our country's history. On February 10, 2007, 146 years after Fort Sumter surrendered and the American Civil War began, Barack Obama announced his first presidential campaign in Abraham Lincoln's hometown of Springfield, Illinois. In that speech, Obama declared that, like Lincoln, he intended to "free a people" and transform a nation.[13]

Well, he did free his people, and there's more crime, more murder, more mayhem. He certainly transformed the nation until Trump came along, and now they're transforming it again. We're today living in a nation more divided than at any time since Lincoln's presidency, and we've entered a time and place that might be as dangerous as it was during those years. As in Lincoln's time, we are not moving toward expanded freedom but toward civil war.

I fear the worst. Let me be clear that while Joe Biden is the executive head of the current administration, I am speaking in broader terms than simply about the president alone. I am speaking about Democratic and Republican senators and congressmen who are doing nothing to hold back a government that has, in my opinion, overreached its legal and constitutional powers and brought us under its control.

Look at what happened with COVID-19. The government is moving more and more toward a nation based not on the rule of law but on greed and hunger for power like a crony oligarchy. Think Nancy Pelosi. A civil war would actually enable this crony government to consolidate the power it has already granted itself through the broad use of executive orders, which is what Biden has been doing day and night. This is a power now granted to cabinet secretaries and other political appointees. And our lawmakers are unwilling to step in and put a halt to this takeover.

You know that with our nation so divided the government could marshal all of those on its side: the IRS, TSA, street gangs of thugs, Black Lives Matter, the National Guard, and our military, which is now being purged of patriots and lacks a real command structure that is loyal to the Constitution. The government could marshal all of those against those who would stand up in oppression.

You should be very frightened right now because something much like what we face today actually happened during Lincoln's presidency. Lincoln was not a saint. As great as he was, he committed crimes against the Constitution and against ordinary citizens. In an 1862 proclamation, Lincoln declared that "since rebels and insurgents in the southern states had created an insurrection, Now, therefore, I, Abraham Lincoln, President of the United States, do hereby proclaim and make known to all whom it may concern that the privilege of the writ of habeas corpus is suspended throughout the United States."[14]

How far away are we from Biden doing the same thing, saying that right-wing terrorists and white supremacists have created an insurrection, that they are subject to martial law, and that the right to a writ of habeas corpus is now suspended? Do you think it can happen here?

Lincoln is estimated to have arrested and imprisoned some 20,000 civilians. They were detained without trials during the Civil War. Southern prisoners were held in internment camps under deplorable conditions. At Fort Delaware, more than 2,000 Confederate soldiers died of scurvy and dysentery. Confederate prisoners in the Union camp at Rock Island were tortured by being hung by their thumbs.

Let us pray that Biden does not follow Lincoln's example. But given his record of ignoring the Constitution and rewriting laws with his executive orders, anything is possible with our rogue president. I don't just think it can happen here. As we saw with Lincoln, it *did* happen here.

Now let's look at the economy and see what that has to do with this underlying rumbling of a civil war. We have a fragile economy. Don't be fooled, it's not improving. The consumer price index has already set a 40-year high.[15] Inflation is out of control. It's not improving.

The fragile economy is not improving. It could be driven to the brink of collapse. The dollar could be worthless by the bursting of the housing bubble or the stock market. At some point, other nations will likely refuse to buy the U.S. Treasury bonds, which have long ensured that the U.S. dollar remained the currency on which the world's economy is built. The consequences will not be good for any of us.

This means that the dollar will likely continue to lose value. Prior to 2014, virtually all international sales of oil were settled in U.S. petrodollars. In 2018, China, one of the largest importers of oil, began settling its foreign oil purchases in yuan, its own currency.[16] At the same time, other so-called BRICS (Brazil, Russia, India, China, and South Africa) nations also announced plans to get off the petro-dollar.[17] The United States, which imports more foreign goods than anyone else in the world, has a lot to lose if the dollar loses value in the world market. It could mean that Americans would have to spend a lot more to import less. We're basically importing inflation with every purchase of foreign goods.

Now the government tries to hide this deficiency with three-card monte statistics. Government inflation charts no longer include such items as food and gasoline and wage stagnation in their calculations. If we measured inflation the way we did in the late 1970s, we'd see that inflation is worse than it was then. Just look at your dwindling bank account and tell me if you think I'm wrong.

As our economy is being challenged, so are our freedoms. The National Security Agency (NSA) is continuing its hostile takeover of Americans' privacy. The technology and storage capacity of the NSA are nearly limitless. Information about your everyday activities is captured and stored in the million-square-foot Federal Data Center in Bluffdale, Utah, in the form of metadata.

Are they monitoring the communications of suspected terrorists in order to prevent them from staging another attack on this country? Sure. But they're also monitoring you. They're monitoring anyone they consider to be a right-winger, a nationalist. Did you understand what I just wrote? All private information, including personal photographs that you send to the cloud, is being stored. In addition to collecting, storing, and distributing our medical and financial records as part of the Affordable Care Act, the IRS has become the arbiter of political speech in the United States.

But what else is going to happen? We're in the midst of a military, economic, and cultural collapse that is turning us into a country in danger of catastrophic failure and could be leading to the night-marish scenario of a civil war. And I fear that with our international power and influence weakened dramatically under Biden, both Republican and Democratic plutocrats could seize control of the political process while the will of the people goes unheeded because conservative voices are increasingly being shut down, drowned out, and erased, whether it's on social media or anywhere else.

Civil war is the most dangerous and destructive event that can occur in any nation and invariably involves atrocities committed by both sides against their own fellow citizens. Such atrocities could happen here.

Let me go back to the American Civil War in August 1863. You may have heard of Quantrill's Raiders operating at that time. They were a band of rebel Confederate soldiers. They attacked the town of Lawrence, Kansas. They massacred 200 men and boys and stole hundreds of thousands of dollars from the townspeople.

In an 1864 battle, the Fort Pillow Massacre occurred. More than 300 African-American soldiers were killed by Confederate troops, many as they stood weaponless with their hands raised. And after the garrison had surrendered, Union soldiers were equally murderous.

In early September 1864, the city of Atlanta surrendered to Union General William Sherman. What happened next? Some 14,000 residents, mostly older men, women, and children, watched helplessly as the "good" troops of the Union under Lincoln's General Sherman burned Atlanta to the ground. Only 10 percent of Atlanta's buildings escaped the inferno.

In the weeks and months that followed, Sherman's troops marched to Savannah, Georgia, leaving behind a swath of destruction 40 miles wide across Georgia. Buildings were burned, family farms pillaged, and innocents murdered.

Lincoln's reelection that November came on the wings of Sherman's supposedly glorious victory. Sherman's march might have been the most unholy act perpetrated on the American people by one of its own in its history. When voices rose in outrage, even some from the North, Lincoln not only turned a deaf ear, but he ordered the censoring of news stories. And a compliant Associated Press acquiesced.

And now, some 160 years later, a situation very similar to the one we faced before the Civil War is taking shape in America. While we're still enjoying what we think is peace, there are subterranean rumblings that portend danger ahead. Look at Minneapolis. The outrageous acts of the left to which you are becoming numb remind me of the months and years before the outbreak of the actual Civil War. I'll repeat again the words of Thomas Corwin to Abraham Lincoln in January 1861: "I cannot comprehend the madness of the times. Treason is in the air around us everywhere. It goes by the name of patriotism."

This is what Black Lives Matter says. They're patriots. They're just defending black people while they loot and burn. The state of our union is in the most perilous position it has been in since the 1860s. We are under assault from both inside and out as our government moves to consolidate its domestic power while at the same time weakening our defenses against the growing power of global enemies like China. All the while, the progressive liberal government–media complex watches the storm clouds gather with few keystrokes of reportage, outrage, or resistance. We've come to a situation that may threaten our very existence as a nation.

CHAPTER 2

THE PUPPET PRESIDENT PLOT

Somewhere deep within the controlling elements
of this government are those who actually run things.
God only knows who they are.
Why would they be doing this to us right now?

NORTHERN CALIFORNIA WAS IN decline for many years. Between the bums in the streets and the crime, it was hard to believe that a city like San Francisco, which once had been so beautiful, had degenerated so rapidly. But I had seen it coming. I saw the corruption of Nancy Pelosi. I saw the corruption of Dianne Feinstein. I saw the corruption of the mayor and the supervisors and tried to warn people. But the people were unmoved.

The people called me every name under the sun: fascist, racist, white supremacist. Eventually, they all realized that they were wrong, that I was right, but the city had fallen so fast so far that they couldn't even reckon what had happened to them, nor did they know who to blame.

Of course, they should have blamed themselves because I had told them for decades that ultra-tolerance would kill them. Once you start tolerating anything, you start to tolerate everything.

WHEN ANYTHING GOES, EVERYTHING GOES

It started with gay rights. That wasn't enough. Then it became gay marriage. Then, anyone opposed to gay marriage was considered a homophobe. After they got gay marriage, it became transgender rights. When even that is not good enough for the far-left socialists, they will change it to something else. Like openly brainwashing very young children into believing that sex change surgery may be the right choice for them!

Everything was a new iteration of the same game, and it wasn't really socialism versus nationalism. It was the destruction of civilization itself. This was emerging not only in northern California but also in liberal cities across the United States, with the arrival on the scene of the most incompetent, characterless president imaginable, Joe Biden.

And so I stayed home one day because I couldn't go anywhere. There was no internet. Without the internet, I couldn't even watch television. I couldn't watch the news. I couldn't watch the History Channel. I couldn't watch a cooking show. I couldn't go on my iPhone to a cooking show for my audience. And so I resorted to what I had done for ages—which was to read.

I did not have a large library in the house I was residing in at the time. But strangely enough, about a week before, I had gone through some dusty old files and found some odd books that I was about to throw in the garbage. Among them was one called, *Hitler: The Memoir of the Nazi Insider Who Turned Against the Fuhrer*, by a man named Ernst Hanfstaengl. And someone named Alan Bullock wrote, *Hitler: A Study in Tyranny*. I do not remember any others as successful as these in providing a credible picture of Hitler as a man.

HOW TYRANTS RISE

I couldn't remember where I had gotten the Hanfstaengl book. The dust jacket was ripped. It was published by a small publisher named Arcade Publishing in 2011. It cost 30 shillings at the time (it was a British publication). A note fell out of it that said, "I think you would enjoy this, doctor."

It's a book about Hitler's rise to power from before the abortive Munich putsch of 1923 to his final triumph when he became chancellor—the years when the seeds of his later deterioration began to show in his character. To this, the author, Dr. Hanfstaengl, is a witness of the utmost importance because not only were his relations with Hitler close until Hitler came to power, but after that he was still the Nazi Party's foreign press chief until his escape to Switzerland in 1937.

Hanfstaengl was also one of the few members of the entourage who was able to back his observations with the judgment of an educated man of the world. Hanfstaengl had come to know Hitler when Hitler was a minor provincial political agitator, a frustrated ex-serviceman:

> Awkward in a blue serge suit, he looked like a suburban hairdresser on his day off. His chief claim to notice was his golden voice and his transcendent powers as an orator on the platform of one of his party meetings. Even then, he was so little regarded that the sparse reports of the press did not even spell his name right.

It's an amazing story about the emergence of this marginal figure Hitler at a time when Germany was being torn apart by a battle between the left, meaning the socialists, and the right, meaning the nationalists. What I took away from this book was that we are witness to history reemerging in America along the same lines.

In our case, the internationalists or socialists are the ones who stand for nothing except the destruction of everything about America. They have not yet broken the crosses off the war memorials and the memorial cemeteries, as I predicted 30 years ago, but they will.

The very same kind of vermin, the ACLU, sought to give each border jumper, each illegal alien, $450,000 to reward them for having snuck into America.[18]

I consider the ACLU the most destructive organization in American history. This is an organization more powerful than either of the two parties because none of its operatives is elected. It does not answer to the people. It answers only to the fanatics who send it money, some of whom know that the ACLU stands for decimation of the nation. Others think they're just doing good to protect oppressed people, meaning oppressed minorities.

The ACL brought a lawsuit that sought the aforementioned $450,000 for each illegal alien whose child was separated from them regardless of whether the child was theirs or not. I couldn't believe that this was actually happening. I couldn't believe that we had a president named Biden whose Justice Department, reports said, was considering this but three days later said it was not garbage.[19] Suddenly, whatever the so-called Justice Department decided to do with them, Biden said he was going to agree to.

During a second press conference, Biden said that he had no power over the Justice Department, which is absolute rubbish. Of course, he could stop them. Of course, he could stop that fanatic from Harvard who's the head of the Justice Department. Merrick Garland was happy to sic the FBI on parents who stood up for their children, who were being mentally raped by the radical left and their transgender brownshirts.[20] I suppose that there was nothing Biden could do about that either because, in his mind, the chief executive has no power over executive branch appointees.

In some ways, America today is in a worse place than the Weimar Republic was in the early 1920s when Hitler rose to power. Now, we're lucky that there is no Hitler in this country and none on the horizon. And there's unlikely to ever be a Hitler, thank God. But will there ever be someone who can marshal America to see its greatness, to see the wonders that America has done for the world without catering to the radical black community, radical Hispanic community, black supremacists, and Hispanic supremacists? Is there anyone who could tell the world the truth?

I asked myself every day for more than 25 years if there was anyone who could marshal the people. I wrote so many great books. One of them comes to mind right now, which is *Scorched Earth: Restoring the Country after Obama.* You can change the name to *Restoring the Country after Biden,* but I don't know if there will be a nation after this administration is finished. I do not know whether the chaos that is Biden's legacy and the destruction that he is sowing can ever be stopped.

I use Anderson Cooper as the example of the worst tendencies of the American media fraud. He is through and through a shallow monster of a human being who pretends that he is thoughtful. And yet all he has is hatred for this nation and everything it stands for. If we had a legitimate media, this would not be happening. The end of Western civilization is no longer a vision for enemies within and without. It is operational. They are doing it. The players are well known, filled with contempt for success and tradition, pandering to the manufactured cry of diversity in order to divide this once great nation.

What is their real goal? Is it equality? Is it equity? No, we have that. Those who can do, those who have anything to offer, succeed. But the left wants to consolidate power forever in their corrupt oligarchy.

Aging film star Alec Baldwin shot someone and killed her on a movie set. And what did newspapers like *USA Today* do? They went into overdrive with propaganda, trying to create sympathy for Alec Baldwin. The headline? "Alec Baldwin and the Neglected Trauma of Unintentional Killing."[21] In other words, he's the victim now.

This is how powerful the filth and garbage in Hollywood is. I have tried to warn you about it for years. Hollywood has tried to destroy me, and it has impeded me in many ways. But here I am. I'm still here. I'm still standing. But, the fact of the matter is that the degenerates in Hollywood behind Alec Baldwin have tried to turn him into a victim just as the powerful filth at HBO and the powerful agencies that run the other networks and run those concerts are protecting the lowlife street rapper who incited a riot from any culpability whatsoever.

The media are so all powerful that people do not know which way to turn. I've seen this filth rise to the point where I don't know if the nation can be saved. Sometimes art imitating life teaches us lessons. That's the universe we're living in now.

Neville Chamberlain was not a wartime consigliere. Germany was on the move. Hitler was invading. Hitler had built up his military, even though others said that he couldn't. That's China right now. And this good-natured weakling, Chamberlain, the pacifist socialist intellectual, came back with an agreement that he couldn't wipe his nose with as far as Hitler was concerned. That was Chamberlain.

Biden is worse than Chamberlain, except that he's not a good-natured weakling. He's a bad-natured man. But he has taken upon himself the passive socialist intellectualism of "Chamberlainism." Back in England, though, Chamberlain's own party got rid of that quisling English leader. That's the benefit of a parliamentary system. We don't have such a system here. We're stuck with this loser for his whole four-year term at the very least.

WHO IS REALLY RUNNING AMERICA?

Somewhere deep within the controlling elements of this government are those who actually run things. Are they with the World Economic Forum? Is it Obama? God only knows who they are. Why would they be doing this to us right now? I could probably give you a short list of those who I think are really running things, although I'm not completely sure who they are. But even they at a certain point must recognize that a nation can be destroyed from within and that they've gone too far by putting this semi-senile incompetent in the White House. Biden has broken free of their controls just as others have done throughout history who were first put into power by more powerful people before going rogue on them.

It happened in Germany. It's not a direct comparison, but if you remember the story of Hitler, who I am talking about, if you read about him, he did not come to power on his own or in a vacuum. Very powerful industrialists backed him in the beginning—the groups, for example, that had been bankrupted after World War I, like the armaments manufacturers. They backed Hitler because they knew he'd be good for business.

Dwight D. Eisenhower warned us to beware of the military–industrial complex. Remember that the same elements are still here in America. There are certain people who wanted Biden in the White House. You know them—George Soros, John Kerry, Nancy Pelosi. They figured that they could always control him. And now he's gotten so crazy and so senile that he's gone off the reservation.

I thought that Biden was unelectable back in 2016. In my book, *Scorched Earth*, I wrote:

> I had a little thought about Biden, by the way. You know
> that he was not electable. His inane off-the-cuff comments

were deadly. Mentally, he's not all there. Remember, I
wrote this in 2016. Mentally, he's not all there. He was
never going to step in during the 2016 election if Grandma
couldn't make it to the finish line. Do you want to know the
only reason they are still warming him up in the bullpen? I
cannot finish this without risking a great deal. But I had a
shocking thought. It's that the rogue president has broken
free of his handlers. That's as far as I can go with that. The
rogue president has gone so far to the left that his handlers
may need someone to keep the nation from going
completely down the drain.

That was in 2016. And here we are today in this year of Our Lord
2023. Bernie Sanders, a naked communist, has spawned millions of
fools like Occasional Cortex and the so-called Squad who are worse
than rotting squid on a kitchen floor. And yet these evil fools are dic-
tating to this deranged administration which way the wind blows.

Still, I wonder who is really pulling the strings attached to this
senile old man.

OPEN SKIES: IS BIDEN
A BEIJING CANDIDATE?

If Biden had been president when Japan attacked Pearl Harbor in
1941, we'd all be speaking Japanese. In addition to open borders, we
now have open skies under this clownish pathological liar. Everyone
knows that the Chinese surveillance balloon that was allowed to
traverse a vast swath of our airspace in February 2023 should have
been shot down over the Aleutian Islands rather than off the coast
of South Carolina.[22] Anyone with a minimal education understands
that.

When that fiasco first started, I put out a tweet asking if Biden was a "Manchurian candidate."[23] Forgive me for my excesses. But I tend to think in a different way than people in the news business. Maybe I jump to conclusions, but I'll ask the question: Is he a Manchurian candidate? He ordered the military to shoot the spy balloon down after it had ample opportunity to send all the data back to Beijing. In other words, he told the farmer with the gun to shoot the fox after the fox had eaten the chickens.

This is equivalent to something Obama did. I was still on the radio at the time and both wrote and talked about it. Back in 2011, the Obama administration sent the shiniest newest drone in our arsenal to land in Iran without a scratch on it, like a new Buick in the showroom.[24] That's not how the Obama administration sorority described it, but it is for all intents and purposes what happened.

Where do you think Iran became so advanced in the drone business? It's from our technology. This party called the Democrat Party is a party filled with traitors from top to bottom. Perverts, criminals, and traitors.

Now, I know I'll be stepping on some toes here, and I don't want to do that, but let me tell you what's even worse than Obama handing them one of our drones: They don't have to shoot down drones. They don't have to have balloons over our bases. They could just read it in our military books. I've been a member of the Navy League for years, and they send me magazines that I look at with wonderment. They list every piece of military equipment the U.S. Navy has.

It lists the locations of all our bases and how many planes and ships are located at each one. It shows virtually every one of our pieces of U.S. Navy in significant detail. It shows the location of all our strike fighter squadrons and the number of planes in each.

It also lists airborne radar systems. It's complete with pictures and quite a few details for our friends around the world.

Remember, I didn't steal this book. I got it in the mail. It was sent to me because I'm a member of the Navy League. I'm sure that there are spies in America who also receive this book. It even includes pictures of our military leadership, as well as their names and where they live, all the way up to the commander-in-chief himself, Joey Biden. Our adversaries can only find such pictures encouraging.

And then there's the genius, Secretary of Defense "Lord" Austin himself. I don't call him Lloyd Austin. He's Lord Austin. This is a nightmare scenario people should not forget or say it's yesterday's news. The Chinese spy balloon first appeared over the Aleutian Islands. How did it even get that far? If it was a Russian satellite, it would have been shot down, wouldn't it have? Then why did we let a Chinese satellite make it to the Aleutian Islands without being shot down?

For that matter, what about the communist dictator of Canada? I call him "False-dough" rather than Trudeau. Why didn't the Canadian military shoot it down?

So Biden shoots down the balloon with a missile, potentially destroying all useful information inside the balloon and on the balloon's equipment. So you can't even reverse engineer it. You risk losing the spy data.

So that's one potential explanation for why he waited. If you want to go paranoid or want to write a novel, you couldn't come up with a better plot. You have a Manchurian candidate owned by the communist Chinese. They tell him, "Shoot it down after it passes through the United States. Make believe you don't know anything about it." I don't think Biden could get through a game of solitaire at this point.

None of this "flies" with the American people. Even the spokes-mouths in the media were asking questions. So Joe's handlers gave him a new line. He said he authorized the military to shoot it down when it was safely over water. And Lord Austin said, "[A]s soon as the mission could be accomplished without undue risk to American lives under the balloon's path."[25]

If Lord Austin is so concerned with American lives, he should be paying more attention to the southern border. As gang bangers and fentanyl pour into the country, Lord Austin, that's what you should be worried about. It's a nightmare from top to bottom. Open skies, open borders. And it's Biden himself who's in charge of all of this. He may be a Manchurian candidate, in my humble opinion. Or perhaps Beijing candidate is more accurate for the times. And if they didn't use the conditioning methods portrayed in the film, maybe they're using the traditional method—bribery?

But maybe it's just plain old corruption. Maybe we have a president whose family is so financially connected in China, Ukraine, and other areas of the world where U.S. interests are at stake—although they shouldn't be in Ukraine—that the president of the United States is unable to effectively represent the American people's interests.

That is the real nightmare scenario.

CHAPTER 3

THE SHOW TRIALS PLOT

———

That America is in any way white supremacist is pure gaslighting. In a white supremacist society, it would not be the white people who had to watch what they said. There wouldn't be minimum quotas for employment or college admission for minorities—there would be maximum quotas.

———

ANY PLOT TO DESTROY America must include destroying our system of justice. I saw this coming back when Biden first seized power. I told you what to expect. I predicted this. I started by describing a dream about the last elephant during my monologue on the inauguration of fear and loathing.

When I woke up that morning, I had a gruesome image that I recalled from my childhood. It was of a grainy black-and-white movie of a tribe of what used to be called "pygmies" deep in the African jungles attacking a noble elephant. I often wondered, how could such small people kill such a large animal?

And then I watched in horror as one snuck up behind the elephant. He jabbed a long spear into its anus, causing unimaginable pain. We could only imagine that as the elephant was distracted by this pain, another pygmy snuck up and stabbed him in the genitals. Another pygmy stabbed him in the eye; then another in the other eye. Then another put a spear in his ear; then another put a spear . . . you get the picture.

Eventually, the poor creature was lying on the ground, moaning, as the pygmies carved it up. One tribesman opened up its guts and pulled out its heart. I woke up in horror that morning thinking of that image from my childhood. It occurred to me that I was watching the death of the Republican Party, if not the death of America itself. The Democrat Socialist Communist Party USA is like that tribe of pygmies, I thought to myself.

I wondered if this image was too gruesome for my audience. But they needed to hear it to understand that what may be coming for them is far worse. You can judge for yourself as I try to make you understand what Biden, Harris, Pelosi, Schumer, and Occasional Cortex would like to do to us. Never forget who they are and what they intend to do.

Biden was inaugurated that day, and although the liars would like you to perceive him as very mild and middle of the road, he's not really mild and middle of the road, as I said in Chapter 1. Forget his persona and what he said and realize what he did.

Biden's first act, even before the inauguration, was to slap everyday ordinary Americans right in the face by nominating an incompetent transgender person as assistant secretary for health at the U.S. Department of Health and Human Services.[26] Why do I say an incompetent transgender person? As the Secretary of Health for the State of Pennsylvania, Dr. Rachel Levine sent the elderly into nursing homes to die of COVID-19.[27] Picking an incompetent transgender person was just the beginning.

The supposed moderate also put a bust of Cesar Chavez in the Oval Office.[28] Now that's the Oval Office where President Donald Trump put a bust of Winston Churchill,[29] who saved the British and all of Europe from the scorches of Nazism.

Why did this dunce in a mask put a bust of Cesar Chavez from a farm workers' union in the Oval Office? He's trying to appease his Hispanic supporters, including the millions of illegal aliens in this country, who now seem to be the tail that's wagging the dog.

INAUGURAL RIOT ACT

Biden's inaugural address was billed as a speech promoting unity. But if you listened closely, you heard his real intentions for the next four years. The speech was nothing but fear and loathing and an attack on the middle class. He said that the Earth is dying, and that racism is rampant, but the last part was the most fear-inducing of all. He said that it is the rise of political extremism, white supremacy, and domestic terrorism that we must confront and defeat. Do you realize what he's saying? He effectively declared war on the white, heterosexual, Christian male who loves the flag.

That was Joe Biden's message to the 74 million of us who did not vote for him. If you are conservative, you are an extremist, a white supremacist, and a domestic terrorist. And he and the evil Democrats are out to get you. Get with the program, or we're coming for you. Is this not trying to instill fear in you because of his loathing for you?

You heard in the media and from the Democrats in the days leading up to the election that we need to "deprogram these people," that such people are part of a cult. We must have our thoughts changed. Is this not trying to fill you with fear? Many would call me an extremist for telling you what's going on. But the reverse is actually true. Old Joe Biden and his comrades are the extremists.

The vermin in the media want to portray Biden as a kindly old man saying, "We all need to heal the nation." All the media, all the Democrats, and all of Hollywood were crying while Joe Biden took the oath. One of them likely had a tingle go up and down his or her leg or its leg. They all gave him high marks, even that sneering snob Chris Wallace then at "Faux" News, who said it was the best inaugural speech he'd ever heard: "I thought it was a great speech. I've been listening to these inaugural addresses since 1961. I thought this was the best inaugural address I ever heard."[30]

Meanwhile, could they have just shown a little grace to the out-going president as he was leaving town? Of course not. As President Trump left that morning, they spewed their hatred and showed their loathing for this poor man and his wife:

> He sneaks out early tomorrow, is the only president in living memory to face the legitimate prospect of post-presidential conviction in the Senate and a lifetime ban on holding office and potential federal and state criminal charges in the courts. Other than that, how was the play, Mr. President?
>
> With his business interests cratering at home and across the globe, with a live question in play whether he will be the first president to ever face a lifetime legal ban on him ever running for office again. With even his wife leaving Washington with an approval rating nearly 20 points lower than any other first lady in history. She's the only first lady in history to be viewed on balance negatively by the American public.[31]

This is just a sample of the hatred that came out of their mouths. Did you hear the loathing? This is not reporting. This is not opinion. This is not journalism. This is outright propaganda and hatred. Did you think that they would stop once they had absolute power after Trump was gone? Oh no. They feel emboldened, really emboldened.

Whom did you think they'd go after next? It's you. That's who. It's you. It started almost immediately. The radical left under Joe Biden has actively attempted to make sure that no one who worked in the Trump administration gets a job.

The big corporations are working hand in hand with the administration, assisting the purge. Companies are pulling donations to conservative politicians, but that's only the beginning. They're also on the lookout for their employees' social media accounts. This means that you and anyone who does not agree with the Communist Party USA, excuse me, the Democratic Party USA, will either have to be reeducated by corporations or thrown out of work.

EXECUTIVE DISORDERS

Unsurprisingly, Biden's first acts as president were getting rid of Trump policies that we all supported. Let me break down some of the executive orders Biden signed on his very first day.

Executive Order 13987 is a reversal of a Trump order that forbids "engaging with and strengthening the World Health Organization (WHO)," that fabulous group of deadbeats. This put us back into the WHO and put the WHO in charge of our ongoing COVID-19 response. Dr. Anthony Fauci was named head of the delegation to the WHO's executive board. We can all see what another two years of Fauci has wrought.

The same executive order created a COVID-19 response coordinator position. The first duty listed for this position was "coordinating a government-wide effort to reduce disparities in the response, care, and treatment of COVID-19, including racial and ethnic disparities." That's just what we need, another bureaucrat working on racial issues.

Rejoining the Paris Agreement on climate change isn't technically an executive order, but it is a reversal of Trump's policy.[32] It means that we'll be under the control of international bodies with regard to what we can do in this nation. This is a big one—and absolutely stupid. What he did next. He revoked the Keystone XL pipeline

permit plus other environmental actions. Let's look at them carefully because I may agree with some of them.

Executive Order 13990 is called "Protecting Public Health and the
Environment and Restoring Science to Tackle the Climate Crisis."
To me, the climate crisis is the hot air coming out of his mouth. He
says the order will create good union jobs. What it will really do
is advance communism, environmental justice communism, while
reversing the previous administration's economic growth policies.
And as far as "reestablishing the Interagency Working Group on
the social cost of greenhouse gases," I don't know what that means.
Nobody does. It's a boondoggle for insiders. Revoking the presidential permit for the Keystone XL pipeline just helped make oil prices
go up. I told my audience at the time that I expected gas prices to
go through the roof by the following summer. I was right.

Next, there's a racial thing rescinding Trump's 1776 commission
plus advancing racial equity for all. What does that mean? This is a
vinyl sign executive order designed to embed equity across federal
policy, rooting out systemic racism. That's a bunch of crap. Does
anyone even understand what he's talking about?

Executive Order 13985, "Advancing Racial Equity and Support
for Underserved Communities through the Federal Government,"
provided more gobbledygook study methods to federal agencies
to create equity. How much more affirmative action taking jobs
from white males do they want? To head this up as domestic policy
advisor, Biden appointed Susan Rice.[33] You remember, she's that
doll who lied for Obama about the Benghazi attack and unmasked
General Michael Flynn as part of the conspiracy to throw the Trump
presidency to Russia.[34]

Executive Order 13986, "Ensuring a Lawful and Accurate
Enumeration and Apportionment Pursuant to the Decennial

Census," is particularly awful. What it really will do is ensure that the Census Bureau counts illegal aliens in the Census. This is in response to Trump having put in a plan to exclude illegal aliens from the Census and apportionment. This means that we'll have Democrats for the next thousand years preserving and fortifying the DACA program.

Biden's order ending the Muslim travel ban is a beauty.[35] Trump's policy barred entry into the United States of people from primarily Muslim and African countries. The action instructs the State Department to restart visa processing for those affected.

So Biden's going to flood the country now with Muslims from Africa and the Middle East. I hope you all sleep better tonight. Setting civil immigration enforcement policies, what does that mean?

Biden also directed the Department of Homeland Security to set "civil" immigration enforcement policies in a reversal of the Trump administration's order that directed harsh and extreme immigration enforcement. In other words, Biden's going to open the floodgates to any illegal who wants to come in by terminating border wall construction. That's great. We don't need a wall. While Trump didn't get much done anyway, he talked about it, so that's no change at all. And after all, we need the flow of drugs into Hollywood and the rest of America, don't we?

Prohibiting workplace discrimination based on sexual orientation and gender identity that's already protected, the order will direct the United States to take all lawful steps to protect the rights of LGBTQ+ individuals. They are already protected. What more do we need? Ordering appointees to sign ethics pledges means that all appointees in the union must sign with the goal of restoring/maintaining ethical behavior—that means nothing.

Next, there's an executive order designed to improve and modernize regulatory review, whatever the hell that means. Biden's executive order was meant to revoke the needless obstacles set forth by the Trump administration's regulatory order. I guess he wants more regulations and more red tape. After all, he's a Democrat, right?

Well, there it is. I guess the biggest order was the one eliminating the Keystone XL pipeline to make sure that our oil prices go through the roof and we're more dependent on Iran and other Middle Eastern nations that are not our friends. And, of course, that is exactly what happened.

THE AMERICAN STASI

When I saw Biden saying that he's creating a unit focused on domestic terrorism,[36] I said, "Where the hell is the Republican Party, squashing this before it gets out of hand?"

I studied the Stasi, the East German Ministry for State Security. It's a nightmare when you see that these people in the Biden administration are creating the exact same type of unit as the Stasi. The Stasi's motto was "*Schild und Schwert der Partei*" (Shield and Sword of the Party). It had a very similar theme to the KGB motto.

This is what Biden created. Everyone will be a domestic terrorist, and if the left is happy about it today, they won't be happy about it tomorrow because, as the world learned during the French Revolution, they only began by killing the counterrevolutionaries. But then the thirsty machine that cut off heads wanted more blood, so they started accusing each other, and then they cut off the heads of people of their own party.

Once this starts, it never stops. Where are the First Amendment attorneys—the big mouths that we heard from for 25 years? Where's the ACLU? You know where they are? They're holding up the government of Florida for $50,000 per illegal immigrant. That's where that criminal organization is.

Anyone bringing in tens of thousands of illegal aliens, many of whom are infected with diseases, is committing domestic terrorism by every definition. Wouldn't you think an organization like the ACLU that showed support for $450,000 per family for illegal aliens is committing domestic terrorism?[37] It's sort of like the mafia holding up the country.

So who's a domestic terrorist? Under the Stasi, there were enemies everywhere. If a child threw a ball over the Berlin Wall, the Stasi investigated the family to find out why. If a light bulb fell out of a window in East Germany, the Stasi investigated the family to see who threw the light bulb out the window. If you doubt that this is where we're headed, I have news for you. We're already there.

NO-BORDERS BIDEN

So there is a domestic front to the war, and there is the war on our borders. I wrote in a previous book that ancient emperors used to march populations out of nations they conquered and march other alien populations in. The Babylonian Exile documented in the Old Testament was just one example of this.

The Soviet Union and other communist countries adopted this practice in the twentieth century. One example was forced deportations from Ukraine by the USSR, which was in addition to the "dekulakization" I described previously. The native Ukrainian population that was deported or killed was replaced by waves of ethnic Russian immigrants into Ukraine, creating the situation you see there today.

The communists perpetrated these atrocities for the same reason ancient emperors did. They wanted to break resistance to their rule stemming from native connections to the land and love of country. Today's globalists are doing the same thing to the United States and Europe. They dupe the population into supporting this tyrannical scheme by whipping up sympathy for the destitute migrants, many of whom are worthy of sympathy but whom American simply cannot support in unlimited numbers.

CHILDREN IN CAGES

When Trump was president, all we saw were pictures of children in cages. That's all you heard from the vermin on the left—kids in cages, kids in cages. Well, now we have more than kids in cages. We have a humanitarian crisis on our border that is decimating our language and our culture.

Do you know what the Biden administration means when it talks about humane enforcement of immigration laws? It means freeing tens of thousands of illegal aliens who have been convicted of serious crimes, including many with homicides, sexual assaults, thefts, and kidnappings and more than you can believe of drug and drunk-driving convictions here in America. Obama allowed more than 36,000 convicted criminals who should have been deported to return to America's streets at that time.[38]

If you've listened to my radio show or podcast over the years, you know the importance I place on my motto on borders, language, and culture. And as you know, by now the Biden administration has done more to further the left's war against America by attempting to destroy these three foundational pillars of our Republic than any administration in our history besides Obama.

When I speak to you about protecting our borders, language, and culture, I speak to you as a first-generation American. My father was an immigrant. My ancestors did not come over on the

Mayflower. They came over from Russia in third-class steerage. They worked hard and died young. They learned to speak English, and they learned America's ways. They did not riot. They did not steal. They were true American immigrants. They joined the melting pot.

But the so-called immigrants of today are not the same as the immigrants of yesterday. I understand that the situation is different now than it was 100 years ago, but the fundamentals of immigration are the same. You come as a guest to a nation and then you must exhibit compliance and determination until you can earn your full-time status.

This is not the immigration formula under the Biden administration. Its idea of immigration is to grant amnesty to those who have crossed our borders illegally. They are, in fact, bringing them in by the hundreds of thousands.

Now I oppose amnesty for many reasons. First, we need to guarantee national security. Not all terrorists fly into the United States on jets. Some of them make their way to Mexico and then walk into this country. This is one of the main reasons I oppose amnesty. We must slam the borders closed *now*. Trump tried to do it, and he was called every name under the sun.

What about the people in this country who are not being taken care of while we are giving cash grants to illegal aliens? This is being done across America by illegitimate Democratic governors. We can look at the overcrowded detention centers. We can see that the illegals are overwhelming many of our emergency rooms and schools, and we know that almost all new immigrants are aligned with liberals and socialism. This means more votes for Nancy Pelosi's party.

Now I don't see these people as "aliens" but as human beings. Many of them are good people with churchgoing, strong families. But I still say amnesty will destroy America. The biggest victims will be poor Americans who are already here, white and black alike. This is the situation we're heading for.

THE WHITE SUPREMACY MYTH

I think a lot of people believe that white supremacy is just when a white person doesn't like a black person, but that's just prejudice in America. White supremacy is a system that codifies special legal privileges for white people that are not enjoyed by the rest of the population. We don't have that here. In fact, we have the opposite. Nonwhite people enjoy privileges through affirmative action, despite the recent Supreme Court decision, that white people do not.

That America is in any way white supremacist is pure gaslighting. In a white supremacist society, it would not be the white people who had to watch what they said. There wouldn't be minimum quotas for employment or college admission for minorities—there would be maximum quotas.

If you want to see a society where one ethnicity has legal supremacy over another, just take a look at Malaysia. You don't get into trouble there for not admitting enough of the minority Chinese population. You get in trouble for admitting too many. That's how any racial supremacy society really works.

With CNN and the rest of the media vermin giving Black Lives Matter a megaphone of hatred, America today is like Cambodia in the 1970s or like Germany in the 1930s, where the Jews were vilified as a matter of form. In San Francisco, the wonderful curator of a museum of modern art who, according to those who worked with him for many years, didn't have a racist bone in his body was forced to resign simply for stating during a meeting that he would continue to collect the work of white people.[39] The media called him a racist and a white supremacist.

A few years ago, I had the pleasure of meeting a gentleman who had a long career as a police officer. He had SWAT team experience and had been a medic, you name it. He had been on the front lines in some of the worst neighborhoods in America.

We got to talking about philosophy, God, and things like that. And he told me some stories of his childhood in the Bronx, New York. One was about an old woman in the neighborhood. I'll call her Mrs. Schwartz. She had a mark on her left arm, not a tattoo, but a mark, and he would ask his mother, "What's that mark on Mr. Schwartz's arm?"

His mother never told him, but he eventually found out. She had been a young girl in one of the European nations overrun by the Nazis. The Nazis came into her village, killed all the men and children, but left all the women alive and raped them. Then they killed them all, or so they thought, and threw them all into a pit, covering them with dirt.

Mrs. Schwartz eventually crawled out of the pit. She was one of only two who survived. She crawled out from the earth, out from the blood, out from the dead people around her and ran into the forest, where she was rescued by Russian communists, who then raped her as well.

That's what the Russians did with all the people they rescued. The girls were raped, but their lives were also saved. The Russians treated their wounds. Mrs. Schwartz became a partisan herself and a fighter. She survived World War II. She moved to New York, got married, and had a family. She had grandchildren. But her life before coming to America was a real tragedy.

Mrs. Schwartz was not a "Karen" of the left. She was not a person talking about a grievance that she herself had never experienced, a fake grievance. She was a victim of real atrocities that we all once agreed we should never allow to happen again.

Well, it is happening again. We're just in the early stages. What happened to Mrs. Schwartz isn't the way persecution of the Jews in Germany or the *kulaks* in the Soviet Union began. First, there was the harassment period. There were many years of demonization of these ethnic groups within those totalitarian societies before the imprisonments, forced deportations, and mass murders began. This is why the mass murder of Jews by the Nazis was called the "final solution"—because there were earlier stages of persecution.

We are in the early stages here of persecution against the traditional American population of European ancestry. We're in the demonization stage, the harassment stage. It's the early stages of a war that was declared on white middle-class America during Joe Biden's inaugural address. If the Democrats get their way, we will be the new *kulaks*, just like in Stalin's Ukraine, persecuted into a minority as our country is seeded with an alien population that will support indefinite rule by the Democrats.

They want to make all of America into California, where the pilot program has already succeeded. They must be stopped.

BIDEN LYNCHES WHITE AMERICA

In February 2023, President Biden hit a new low. This is something we would have expected from the vile mouth of Al Sharpton or the hijack artist Jesse Jackson. They have been doing it to America for four decades. We have not seen a president divide America like this since Barry Obama came along and did so on a daily basis. I'm talking about Biden's remarks while attending the screening of a film about Emmet Till, a black teenager who was murdered in Mississippi in 1955. He took the opportunity to lecture us further about the history of lynching and celebrate the 2022 bill making lynching a hate crime.[40]

As far as I know, lynching has been outlawed for a very long time. I don't know of a time in American history when homicide was legal. So why would this lowlife in the White House feel the need to say that "white families gathered to celebrate the spectacle" of lynching? What is he trying to achieve by this? He said that white people took pictures of the bodies and mailed them as postcards.

I don't know whether that's true. But why would he talk about a thing like that at a time like this when the country is at the point of a civil war? What does he hope to achieve other than more violence against white people?

There is a war going on right now on a very low level. And if you look at most of the acts of violence going on in America today, look no further than New York City. Look no further than the subway murders and who is committing them. It's not white people lynching black people. It's deranged homeless people, mainly African American. Look at the real data on who is conducting this war of terror against not only white people but also Asian people and *other black people*.

The FBI releases data on hate crimes every year. For 2019, there were 6,406 hate crime offenders. And 52.5 percent of them were white, 23.9 percent were black or African American, 14.6% were of unknown race, and the remaining 9 percent were of other races. American Indian or Alaskan Native comprised just over 1 percent, while Asians were not even 1 percent.[41]

Of course, the left will screech that this proves that white people commit most of the hate crimes, but that's not true. Conveniently for the left's narrative, the FBI's totals for "whites" includes Hispanics, even though they are considered "people of color" for all other purposes. The same FBI report indicates that Hispanics made up 10 percent of the 5,443 offenders for whom "ethnicity" was reported.[42]

So if you simply apply that percentage to the overall number, it turns out that non-Hispanic whites make up just 42.5 percent of the offenders—less than half—despite comprising 59.3 percent of the population. Hispanics commit 10 percent of the hate crimes while comprising 18.9 percent of the population.[43] So, whether you count them together or separately, whites and Hispanics represent a significantly smaller percentage of hate crime offenders than their percentage of the general population.

Blacks, in contrast, represent 23.9 percent of hate crime offenders compared with their mere 13.9 percent share of the population.[44] Blacks are the only group whose share of hate crime offenders exceeds its share of the population—and it's almost double. This generally lines up with the numbers on crimes in general. So which racial group is the real problem?

Regardless, why would Biden attack white people at a time like this? My best guess is he's so senile that he's a puppet. They put a script in front of him. He has no judgment left at all. I learned in graduate school that the first thing to go in the elderly is judgment. Biden's is obviously gone. He is a mere mouthpiece.

The question is, who would write this and put it in front of him? What could be gained from talking about white people lynching black people 150 years ago? Is there another plausible reason besides instigating more violence in this country?

Doesn't Biden already own the black vote? We're supposed to believe that he got even more black votes in 2020 than Barack Obama in either of his election wins. How many more black people can he get to vote for him, and how many intelligent black people want to be pandered to like this? I can't imagine too many. So, what is he trying to do here but stir up more hatred?

America is at a tipping point. It's hanging in the balance like a loose tooth. And this man is not fit to be the dentist for the future of this nation. If ever there was a reason to impeach this senile old coot, it is now. In a sane nation, the Republican Party would say enough is enough. We're going to impeach Joe Biden. It's time to remove him.

The problem is that someone even worse than him is waiting in the wings. They've set it up so that we can't impeach him. Every word out of Kamala Harris's mouth is about racial enmity and hatred. But with Harris you get that imbecilic giggle afterwards. We're in very deep trouble right now, and I don't know that the country can survive until the end of this administration.

So, it's like him shooting down a $15 hobby balloon with a $400,000 Stinger missile. He is trying to shoot down what's left of America's integrity, both domestically and around the world. Talking about lynching is something we have come to expect from leeches and race hustlers like Al Sharpton and Jesse Jackson but not from a man who holds the highest office in the land.

BLACK COMMUNIST ANGELA DAVIS'S WHITE PRIVILEGE

Imagine fighting for something your whole life just to realize that you've really been fighting against yourself. This is what happened to former Black Panther Angela Davis when she made a shocking discovery about her own ancestry. It turns out that this infamous antiwhite domestic terrorist is actually a descendant of William Brewster, one of the original 101 colonists who came to America on the *Mayflower*.[45]

Davis may look like a friendly grandmother, but she's a monster. She's a terrorist. She's a murderer, in my opinion. This woman supplied the weapons smuggled into the Marin County Courthouse by the Black Panthers who took hostages and eventually blew the head off a judge.

This is what Angela Davis did. She served only a few months in jail. And then the vermin in California rewarded her with tenured professorships for the next 30 years. So don't fall for the nice grandmotherly look. She's a con woman and a monster, a Marxist and a terrorist. But worse than that, she's a hypocrite.

Davis was one of the subjects of an episode of the long-running PBS series, *Finding Your Roots*.[46] During the episode, the show's host, Henry Louis Gates, Jr., tells her that not only did her white ancestor arrive in America on the *Mayflower* but that it was none other than William Brewster, the first religious leader of Plymouth Colony. In fact, Davis has Caucasian ancestry on both her paternal and maternal sides.

In addition to William Brewster, Davis is also a direct descendant of a man named Stephen Darden, who fought in the American Revolutionary War. After the war, written records show that Darden moved from Virginia to Georgia, where he owned a farm and at least six slaves.

Davis's grandfather, her mother's father, was a white Alabama lawyer named John Darden, who was born in 1879. He was a prominent citizen who served in the Alabama legislature and the publisher of a newspaper called *The Goodwater Enterprise*. Of course, Davis's first question about her own grandfather was, "Was he a member of the Ku Klux Klan or the White Citizens' Council?"

Davis's comments made a bell go off in my head. I said, "Wait a minute. That sounds like Black Lives Matter today." You have to pledge support for BLM in order to advance in this country today in academia or corporate culture. It's a nightmare what's going on in this country. And I am sick of it. I think that we'd all like to stand up to them and say, "Go to hell. We're not paying you a dime in so-called 'reparations.'"

I'm an immigrant's son. You'll have to rip it out of my hands, because I'm not paying you a nickel. You owe me reparations, Angela. I'll tell you why. I've lost job after job to less-qualified people of color. I've already paid exorbitant reparation taxes to support welfare, which is disproportionately received by people of color.

Well, surprise, Angela. It looks like you will also be paying reparations instead of collecting them. Or maybe the money will come in on Monday and you'll have to send it back on Tuesday because you'll both be entitled to and responsible for reparations.

Davis's case is by no means the only inconvenient fact when it comes to reparations for slavery. There is also the case of Anthony Johnson, a black man captured by African slave traders and sold as an indentured servant to a Virginia landowner in 1621. He eventually earned his freedom and became a wealthy landowner, owning five indentured servants himself—four white and one black. The black man's name was John Casor.

Here is where the story gets very interesting. Casor served out what he claimed was the term of his indentured servitude and demanded his freedom. Another colonist named Robert Parker accused Johnson of holding Casor illegally, which, if proven, could jeopardize Johnson's land holdings. Johnson released Casor based on this threat, and Parker immediately signed Casor to a new seven-year indenture![47]

Realizing that he had been played for a fool, Johnson sued in court to reclaim Casor and won. In ruling in favor of plaintiff and black man Anthony Johnson, the court made Casor the first person of African descent declared a slave for life in the Thirteen Colonies.[48] So, the first person in what became the United States of America to enslave for life a black man from Africa was another black man from Africa. I suppose that was something your Maoist professors left out of their antiwhite lectures.

Now, of course, I am not suggesting that Anthony Johnson or any other black African American represents the typical slaveowner in nineteenth-century America. Black slaveowners represented a tiny percentage of overall slaveowners. But I think most American liberals would be very surprised to hear that the U.S. Census of 1830 listed almost 4,000 black slaveowners in the United States.[49]

So what about their descendants? Does anyone really believe that the descendants of black slaveowners will be identified and withheld reparations? Of course not. It would be impossible for a government that can barely deliver the mail to perform the complex investigation that Henry Louis Gates, Jr., performed in chasing down the lineage of Angela Davis. Even Gates himself could not run an operation to do investigations like this for tens of millions of people.

I point all of this out to demonstrate the absurdity of attempting to make reparations to an entire race of people based on the injustice done to their ancestors hundreds of years ago. But I don't object to reparations primarily because they're absurd. I object to them because no American of any race alive today has been either a victim or a perpetrator of slavery. Tax-funded reparations for slavery amount to punishing the innocent and rewarding nonvictims.

But let's call it what it really is: buying votes with money stolen from your political opponents. It's just one more way to rig elections going forward in the Democrats' eternal quest to create a one-party America. No thanks!

CHAPTER 4

THE CENSORSHIP PLOT

It is not about conservatives or conservatism.
It's about anyone who expects to continue to have
a voice in America, because when they came for me,
no one raised their voice in my defense. And if this isn't
stopped, then when they come for you, there'll be
no one left to defend you either.

THE VERY FIRST RIGHT guaranteed by the Bill of Rights to our Constitution is the right to free speech. It is the right that makes possible the articulation and understanding of all the others. So it's no surprise that the key feature of the plot to destroy America is destroying free speech. And no meaningful discussion about free speech can avoid what I call the "death of talk." What do I mean by this? I mean the attacks on white people, white males in particular, with a fake narrative about white supremacy and white nationalism. I have news for you. If you think you're not racist, you may be right.

You're supposed to ignore this elephant in the room or risk being erased by the leftist thought police. I refuse to ignore it. Remember, I'm the only one in the American media who's ever been truly canceled on a national level. I was banned in Britain, and I'm still the only person on a blacklist, unable to travel to the United Kingdom, to Britain in particular, because of lies put out about me by the then-left-wing government.

Not one person in talk radio or the media came to my defense. Not one person in the media stood up for me, including many who are worshiped by conservatives. One of them, the biggest fraud of them all, the greatest con man in the history of the media in my estimation, actually went on the air and said I deserved what happened to me. And he poses today as a talk radio host and as a self-described great American. Many conservatives buy the act. So much for conservative talk radio defending its own.

So why am I telling you this? Because I was the canary in the coal mine, so to speak. I was banned from a whole country, and now they want to erase all white people from every country in the West. How does this witch hunt end? Does it end when the guillotine stops falling? Because this is a guillotine that is falling across America right now, although so far blood is not being shed. Not directly, anyway.

I could argue that the rise in violence across America, against whites in the streets and against Asians in the streets, against all who oppose the increasingly fascistic LGBTQ+ agenda is being promulgated by the media and the universities. This is the way all atrocities against demonized groups begin.

First, they pillory you. They spread propaganda against whites, and straight white males in particular. What do they do next? Cancel you. They say, "He said this. He said that," and they throw you off the radio. They take you off television. They fire you from your job. They terminate you from a laboratory, no matter how good a scientist you are. They stop you from flying a plane, no matter how good a pilot you are. They demote you in the military and promote incompetents who have nowhere near your qualifications.

It's happening right now in front of our eyes. I stood firm against an entire government to try to free my name from a list of murderers and terrorists—and I lost. I could not get my name off that list. I had nobody in the media, including all your heroes, come to my aid. But I found secret documents and emails that prove the British government's conspiracy to ruin an innocent man's reputation. I found that information was kept under wraps by both Britain's and America's left media.

I'm reaching out to people of all beliefs right now—people of all faiths, all political stripes, who value their right to free speech and who respect the sanctity of independent thought. It's a matter of survival whether you realize it or not.

It is not about conservatives or conservatism. It's about anyone who expects to continue to have a voice in America, because when they came for me, no one raised their voice in my defense. And if this isn't stopped, then when they come for you, there'll be no one left to defend you either.

This is a worldwide political crisis. It is filled with propaganda cover-ups running rampant in international politics, censorship by the Biden regime now in power in America, a dangerous trend globally that continues to sideline the *vox populi* in favor of dictatorships. It begins with silent approval of dictatorial powers.

First, free speech is removed by canceling people who they say are not good people. Then freedom of assembly is removed under the guise of COVID-19, and then eventually the entire national infrastructure is eroded again. I could compare this to Nazi Germany, as well as to Castro's Cuba and the Soviet Union, to show you how these murderous aspirations begin. They begin with exactly what is going on in America today.

Pay very close attention to what happens if you don't stand up. For those who are banned, it leads not only to the death of talk but also to a genocide against an entire race.

ROGAN, RACISM, AND REALITY

As a podcaster with a fairly large audience, I understand the business very well. And I don't want to be put in the position of defending podcast titan Joe Rogan's saying the N-word. I've never used it in or out of context. One such human tick who is attacking Rogan is radio host Howard Stern—I'd love to see him without his wig.

The leftists attacking Joe Rogan are the same people who snap the crosses from our churches and remove our memorial statues. They're a danger to our survival. There's nothing left of freedom among them. They're relentless in their efforts to disrupt the free flow of ideas. Charges of racism constitute their hammer, but they use it very selectively.

Take Whoopi fake-Goldberg. That's not even her name. She took a Jewish name way back when she started, she said, because Jews ran Hollywood. She claimed that the Holocaust wasn't racist because it was white people killing white people in Nazi Germany. I was shocked by what I heard. Is this woman so dumb that she didn't know Hitler built his entire platform on the "Aryan race" and that the Jews were not part of it? Or is she a racist?

I don't know, but she hasn't been fired. The network suspended her for two weeks.[50] It's suspension with Chapter Seven. As George Orwell wrote in *Animal Farm*, "Some animals are more equal than others."

Neither did they object to the degenerate series *Euphoria*, which is glorified child pornography. No outcry to ban this filth. It's all selective outrage against any conservative, period, end of story.

I've been canceled by Cumulus Media Networks. I had one of the largest radio shows in the country. Everyone knows that I'm not on one radio station today. So I understand what the Fourth Reich looks like, but it's been a long time in the making. It did not start with the attempted cancellation of Joe Rogan or the actual cancellation of Carlson. It started a long time before that with the ACLU.

The ACLU is the head of the snake. I have studied communism, Marxism, and socialism as well as Vladimir Lenin, who reshaped

Russia into a totalitarian state and created a totalitarian regime. Race politics erases historical memory and the racist opposition, much like what we're seeing today in the actions of the ACLU. This is addressed in greater detail in a book I wrote in 2005 called *Liberalism Is a Mental Disorder*. It's not only a mental disorder; it's a war against our survival.

Howard Stern is the worst of the bunch, but he's not the only one to pretend to be a progressive or a left winger, and then a right winger, and then middle of the road. And then, suddenly, he wanted unvaccinated people denied hospital care.[51] What does that say about him?

There are others. What about Bill Maher on HBO? He's used as a cover for their new child pornography, *Euphoria*. But he's making believe the far left has moved him to the center. Leftists like him want you to believe they're centrist. They're not. They're canceling everything. Can you name a real conservative who's had a show on HBO? I had one of the biggest radio shows in the country. Nobody could ever even get me on HBO as a guest.

MEDICAL MARXISM

In 2020, *Medical News Today* published an article titled, "Everything You Need to Know about White Fragility." This idea is being spread through the universities as though it is truth when it is pure racism. There is an entire industry of hate being promulgated as antiracism, promoted under the guise of attacking white supremacist Nazis and Ku Klux Klan members. The perpetrators are so clever that they have devised a strategy that if you get angry at them for saying you are a racist, you're a racist. They say that your "reactions may include anger, fear, guilt, arguing, silence or leaving the stress-inducing situation."[52]

These bad people have the nerve to publish this and then say, "By behaving in this way, white people may prevent people of color from attempting to talk about racism with them." So, when you're attacked as a racist, you can't argue, you can't remain silent, and you can't even peacefully walk away. Anything other than submission to the Maoist struggle session is racism.

They say that white people may experience "racial stress" if anyone claims that their views are racist or even if a "person of color" merely talks about their "racial experiences and perspectives." Other sources of racial stress, according to this piece of propaganda, include the following: "A person of color not protecting a white person's feelings about racism; a fellow white person not agreeing with another white person's perspective on racism; a white person receiving feedback that their behavior or actions had a racist impact; a white person being presented with a person of color in a position of leadership."

This is not medical news. It is pure, unadulterated racism. This is what the Soviets did when they used psychiatric hospitals to jail dissidents. Read *The Gulag Archipelago* by Solzhenitsyn, and you'll see what's going on in this country today. Stand up to these racists, whether they are white or not. Anyone pushing these ideas of white fragility, white supremacy, or white guilt is a racist by definition.

The article goes on to say, "Although white fragility is not racism, it may contribute to racism by dismissing white domination and racial conditioning by developing racial stamina." These are insane people. I'm sick and tired of listening to this. They're taking the best minds of our generation, targeting them, and destroying them. It is happening in the schools, in the universities, and in the corporations—wherever you turn.

Where did this come from, this whole idea of white fragility? It was invented by a person named Robin DiAngelo, who has a PhD in so-called multicultural education. Her specialty is whiteness studies and critical discourse analysis, which is a total invention.

Can you imagine someone creating a course on blackness studies or studies about the hatred of blacks toward other races? Or the hatred of Hispanics toward blacks? Or the hatred of Mexicans toward Americans by calling them gringos? Or the hatred of some Hawaiians calling white people "haoles"?

The term "white fragility" came from a piece written by DiAngelo called *White Fragility: Why It's So Hard for White People to Talk about Racism*. DiAngelo wrote a book on the topic to further push the big lie about how white fragility is promoting racism.

The *Medical News Today* article goes on to say, "Racism occurs when white people benefit from an unequal distribution of privileges and people of color experience deprivation." Let's look into this for a minute. What is "an unequal distribution of privileges"? Let's say that you are born into a poor family and grow up in a crime-ridden neighborhood. Your parents kill themselves to save enough money to move out of that neighborhood and move you to a better one where there's less crime, but where there happens to be fewer people of color. This is an example of racism to these people.

In other words, you should all live in a crime-ridden slum in order to be equal. Isn't that what they're saying? This definition of racism, by the way, only applies to white people because of white privilege. This is the most racist statement in the article.

This is something out of the Soviet Union.

"ACADUMBIA"

I warned you years ago on my radio show that once unqualified people were put into universities and they could not keep up with real, demanding academics, they would invent departments like ethnic or gender studies, write papers, and give themselves awards. And then they would start to take over the whole university system with these fallacious arguments.

Let me ask you something: Why were 98 percent of all the great advances and inventions in the world brought forth by white men?

In San Francisco, there is a high school for gifted children called Lincoln High School. And the majority of students who get in based on their grades and performance are Asians. Aren't Asians people of color? Oh no, they're not. Once a racial minority can excel in academics, they're no longer a minority. They are lumped in with evil white people.

So what are they doing about it in San Francisco? They're trying to eliminate schools for children who are smart. They keep trying to do the same thing in New York at the Bronx High School of Science, Stuyvesant, and Brooklyn Tech.

Really smart kids went to those schools. Admission was very difficult. You had to be a whiz kid to get into Bronx Science or Brooklyn Tech. Everyone knew that. Nobody called it racism or segregation, or racial arrogance, or white dominance. We knew they were smarter kids than most of us in math and science, and no one argued against it.

Now you have armies of unqualified people trying to break down the walls of academic excellence in order to destroy any differences between kids. It is the meltdown of excellence in America. Where will our engineers and scientists come from if this garbage is allowed to go unanswered? Where will our future inventions come from if these schools take unqualified kids and mix them in and tell you that everyone's equal?

We all have equal access to education. We all have equal access to books. We all have equal opportunities to exhibit our intelligence.

But this doesn't mean that our native intelligences are the same. Do I have to make the crude analogy of a football field? Why are sports teams dominated by people of color? Because they're better athletes by and large? Is that a racist statement, or is it a simple observation?

Now many of us understand that Asians excel in America because they inherently have a love for learning. They're hard-working people, and frankly, they teach their children to study. It's drilled into them from childhood. So, if you look at the anti-Asian admissions policies going on in America, you will see that the Asians today are the "new Jews."

Now why do I say the new Jews? Because there used to be quotas on Jews in the Ivy League colleges and elsewhere early in the twentieth century? Did you know that they held Jews to much higher admissions standards than applicants from other groups to prevent their rising in the universities? This was done because there were too many successful Jewish children getting into the elite schools and moving ahead, so they discriminated against them?

Now they're doing it to Asians. It's being done in New York by eliminating any differentials in excellent schools such as the Bronx High School of Science or Brooklyn Tech because there are too many Asians. It was done at the University of California at Berkeley. When too many Asians were getting in, they started to discriminate against Asians.

Why is the civil rights community silent on this issue? Because the civil rights community is not a civil rights community. It's a business, and it's a business that's in charge of defending only one or two races. It's not about equality. A federal judge ruled recently that Harvard does not discriminate against Asians. That's a complete lie. Harvard does discriminate against Asians. Asians do not have equal opportunity. The fact of the matter is they must fight even harder than they are now because discrimination is wrong no matter whom it is directed at. And Asian Americans must fight affirmative action and support equal opportunity in order to be given fairness in the college admissions process.

Most first-generation immigrants from China do very well here because they're hard working and they know that everything depends on them. We all know that there are ballot initiatives that make it illegal for the states to discriminate against or grant preferential treatment to individuals based on race, sex, color, ethnicity, or national origin. We know this, but we know it's done all the time, and it's all aimed at attacking whites and Asians. Everybody knows this.

Last April, Democrats in the state legislature of Washington actually overturned that ban of discrimination based on race, sex, and color. Are you listening? Overturn that? Democrats in Washington state said that discrimination is fair game. They did not care what the Asians said. Can you believe this? No matter what the people say?

And so, my friends, equal opportunity must be for everybody. It's not just a slogan. Equal opportunity affirmative action is preferential hiring when universities say that race is only one factor among many considered in the admissions process. What they're doing is stacking the deck against Asians.

A lawsuit was brought against Harvard by a group of Asian students and parents, and their research showed that an Asian-American applicant with a 25 percent chance of admission would have a 35 percent chance if he or she were white, a 75 percent chance if he or she were Hispanic, and a 95 percent chance if he or she were African American. Is this your idea of fairness? No, it isn't. It's discrimination, whichever way you look at it. Quotas are ugly. Preferences are ugly. This is shameless. It's un-American. It's insulting, and it must be fought against. We need equal opportunity in the United States of America.

You must stand up to these racist goons or you will lose not only your nation but also your freedoms.

FRANCE REJECTS MARXIST INSANITY

I told you that this could lead to genocide. But before it leads to genocide, it will lead to the death of our heritage and identity and Western civilization itself. This is obvious to anyone with a brain. The president of France, Emmanuel Macron, figured this out and got together with intellectuals in France and concluded that France is being contaminated by the leftism of America.

The unique way to preserve our democracies is to establish a public and democratic order in this new space where our people think and live. This is one of the critical challenges of our times. Internet platforms were originally allowed to be very politically incorrect. But those same platforms that allowed the people to circumvent the old media gatekeepers and helped President Trump to get his message directly to the people who wanted to hear it suddenly cut the mike or put the mike on mute. They killed all the platforms where it was possible for conservatives to express themselves. This is not a democratic answer.

I don't want to live in a democracy where the decision to cut your mike is decided by a private player, a private social network.

In a speech in October 2020 on the fight against separatism, French President Macron warned against leaving "the intellectual debate to others" as he cautioned about certain social science theories entirely imported from the United States.[53] His education minister, Jean-Michel Blanquer, also warned that there was a "battle to wage against an intellectual matrix from American universities."[54]

France is known for its intellectual capacity; America is not. The French are known for their thinkers; America is not. And the politicians and prominent intellectuals in France, including the president of France himself, are voicing concern that "out-of-control leftism" and "cancel culture" from the United States are threatening French identity and heritage itself—and they're trying to fight it.

The debate over there came to a head after the new director of the Paris Opera, Alexander Neef, published a 66-page report on diversity at the company in which he vowed to diversify staff.[55] He made this promise after five black members of the ballet company circulated an open letter among the Paris Opera's 800 employees calling for greater diversity. In other words, they were being advanced based on their abilities. But they wanted to be advanced because of their race.

Marine Le Pen called Neef's vow "antiracism gone mad,"[56] while the French newspaper Le Monde said, "He soaked up American culture for 10 years while he worked in Toronto."[57] In other words, his mind was warped and poisoned.

French intellectuals also have blamed the suicidal insanity being taught in American universities for Islamic terror attacks. After several such attacks, Education Minister Blanquer said that American universities were complicit because of their stifling of truth telling about Islamist throwbacks. Gilles Kepel, one of a hundred prominent scholars who wrote a letter making the same argument, said that American influence on French culture led to a "sort of prohibition of universities to think about the phenomenon of political Islam in the name of a leftist ideology that considers Islam the religion of the underprivileged."[58]

Historian Pierre-André Taguieff argued in the same way that the "American-style black question" was a "totally artificial importation to France." Now listen to the punch line here: He said that it was all driven by hatred of the West as a white civilization.

"The common agenda of these enemies of European civilization can be summed up in three words," he wrote, "decolonize, demasculate, de-Europeanize…straight white males. That's the culprit to condemn and then to eliminate the enemy."[59]

I warn you that cancel culture in this country, the death of talk in this country, the targeting of white people in this country will lead to genocide and the death of civilization itself. The French realize that out-of-control woke leftism and cancel culture from the United States are a threat to France because they attack the nation's heritage and identity, according to French politicians and intellectuals and the president of France itself.

But it's not just France that's standing up to this anti–white racism. The United Kingdom is as well. Nigel Farage pointed out that Coca-Cola is forcing its staff to take training courses from the very same evil, left-wing radical liberal professor who came up with this whole lie about white fragility and teaching its staff how to be "less white."[60]

Do you have any idea how psychopathically racist this is? How to be less white? Can you imagine teaching a course on how to be less black, how to be less Asian, how to be less Latino? Who would take this? Why don't they all stand up and say, "Drop dead. Go to hell. I'm not doing it"? They don't because they're afraid. Listen to what Farage is saying about Coca-Cola forcing its staff to take training courses on how to be less white. You will not believe it.

Farage also says that this nonsense is being imported into his country from America. He sums it up beautifully when he says, "And the inference here is clear, isn't it? That white is bad; white means supremacist; white means you look down your noses at everybody else; white means you are guilty!"

The Old World does not want anything to do with what the New World is exporting. They realize what it is. It's not about equality; it's not about equity. It's about the death of Western civilization. It's about the destruction of an entire race, which will lead to a holocaust and genocide. This will not end until we all stand up at work and say, "Hell, no, I won't go!"

THE REAL INSURRECTIONISTS

You may think that I'm exaggerating when I say genocide. I'm sure the Jews in 1932 Germany or the Armenians in the 1890 Ottoman Empire thought the same thing. But certainly, you might say, we don't have concentration camps here in America.

No, not concentration camps, but we do have hundreds of political prisoners being denied basic constitutional rights. I'm talking about the hundreds of people imprisoned for being involved in the January 6, 2021, riots. A few of them are violent criminals. The vast majority are guilty of no more than trespassing.

Both the Nazis and the Soviets ran "show trials" to persecute enemies of the state. Sure, there were trumped-up charges against those prosecuted, but they were mainly prosecuted for their political beliefs. This is why most of the "insurrectionists" from January 6, 2021, are rotting in jail.

If you question or challenge an election, you're now an "insurrectionist." So, let's apply it retroactively. This means that most Democrats who challenged Trump's 2016 win would be thrown out of office. These people are insane. They want to give voting rights to illegal aliens. They want to give voting rights to the few prisoners left in Democratic prisons, but they don't want to permit Republicans to run for office. Let me say another thing: The one behind all of this is not Marc Elias. It was likely the Red Queen, Nancy Pelosi.

I remember a number of years ago she gave a graduation speech at the University of California at Berkeley, during which she said to all the graduates, "Be disruptors."[61] She told them to go out there and be a disruptor. Disruptors are good. If these Republicans had any brains and any guts, they would have dug up that speech and throw it in her face.

There are no Republicans fighting this battle properly. They're all dancing around and are running away. Nancy Pelosi was the one doing all of this. Never forget that she is one of the most corrupt politician in the history of America. What about an investigation of insider trading? Where would that go?

I found a French leftist professor who was a communist, Simone Weil, who wrote this: "Whenever one tries to suppress doubt, there is tyranny." Now I'd like to turn this on the liberals. They are suppressing doubt, and they're producing tyranny. You can't doubt the vaccine. You can't doubt what's going on in Washington. So they're producing these rebellions by suppressing any doubt.

What the left itself once believed in has been thrown out the window by what is not really a left-wing government. This is the mistake we're making. The Democrats are not a left-wing or liberal government. They're a gangster regime. They're criminals. Most of them are on the take one way or another. You can look at every one of them, and they have their hands in the pie somewhere.

What they're doing with the January 6 investigation is very cleverly turning it on these poor people who went to Washington on January 6. Some say that government officials are the insurrectionists. They were the ones with the guns. They were the ones who killed an unarmed female veteran. No guns were used by the protesters.

So we have suppression of free speech, the death of talk, the demonization of a specific ethnic group, and show trials. This is being perpetrated by the real insurrectionists, who, like the Bolsheviks in 1917 Russia, are perpetrating a Marxist revolution in broad daylight. How far does this have to go down the terrifying road to genocide before Americans wake up?

CHAPTER 5

THE CULTURE PLOT

I'm an American, and I'm sick and tired
of having to make excuses for the USA.

WHAT IS A NATION? The key elements of a nation are its borders, language, and culture. So any plot to destroy America would seek to undermine all three of these. The plotters have perhaps been most successful in destroying our culture. This goes not only for America but also for all of Western civilization. This is not only rotting our own society from within but also causing conflict on the geopolitical stage.

THE DEGENERATE WEST
VERSUS THE CHRISTIAN EAST

There are many reasons why Putin invaded Ukraine in February 2022. While most of the reasons are geopolitical, I believe that cultural factors are at play, too. I have called it a spiritual and territorial war. And let me make one thing abundantly clear: I am not attempting to justify Putin's invasion in any way. One can try to understand his motives without agreeing with them or how he acted on them. If a man shoots his wife because she cheated on him, the prosecutor is not justifying the shooting by establishing the motive for the crime.

Some people might say that this is a war between the degenerate West and traditional Christians. I would say that this is an over-generalization. But I would also say that there's some truth to it. Putin does not want the perversion of the West to pollute Russia. Not that Russia is pure, but when you consider that Zelensky was a perverse vaudeville comedian who played the piano with his penis on stage to standing ovations, you might understand the revulsion of traditional Russians.

When you see Zelensky's antics, maybe Putin doesn't want the LGBTQ+ agenda invading Russia. Maybe Putin doesn't want fentanyl invading Russia. Maybe Putin doesn't want brainwashing of this type invading Russia.

I think people need to understand the history of the region, which goes back at least a thousand years. This conflict did not begin eight years ago. It did not begin 80 years ago. It began a thousand years ago.

We need to understand who Zelensky is. I believe he is a puppet of George Soros. We also have to understand the mindset of Putin, who is a dictator and a tyrant. But Zelensky has challenged and provoked him for years now, ever since being installed by Soros. Zelensky provoked the Russian bear by sticking him over and over again.

Just before the invasion, Zelensky suggested that Ukraine had a right to consider that the 1994 Budapest Memorandum, under which Ukraine gave up its nuclear weapons, was not working and its provisions were in doubt.[62] In other words, he put the prospect of Ukraine acquiring nuclear weapons on the table. And a U.S. State Department official said that if Putin invades, he'll go home with body bags.[63]

This is not diplomacy.

Now, I must emphasize that both the Ukrainian people and the Russian people have suffered throughout the centuries. But we also must remember that the Ukrainians had Nazi divisions in World War II and the Russians did not.

I am ancestrally from Belarus, which was really part of Ukraine during World War II. All my ancestors, and millions of other Jews, were killed by the Nazis in World War II, and my ancestors actually saw the Soviets as their saviors.

Now, once the Soviets came in, it was not a picnic either. The Soviets also did horrible things. But there were Nazis in Ukrainian divisions, and there still are Ukrainian Nazis. So, when we hear Putin say, I have wanted to take the Nazis out for the last eight years, there must have been Ukrainian Nazis fighting the Russians. It's like World War II all over for them, so they never forget.

Americans like the underdog, whether it's in a sporting match or anything like this conflict—they like the underdog. So, it's natural for them to sympathize with little Zelensky. But he is a terrible man. Not as simple as the little guy faces the big guy.

Again, we have to understand that this is about a thousand years of Russian religious history. Putin says that he wants to recapture spiritual space. This is a terrifying phrase that goes back a thousand years in Russian religious history. Putin sees himself as rebuilding the Soviet Union, which everyone is repeating over and over again like robots, but they have to understand that he's also rebuilding, in his mind, "Holy Russia." It's an extension of the ancient Russian Empire, and unless people understand how Putin thinks, they'll never understand what's occurring.

We have a country that's only a few hundred years old. Russians have a nation that's thousands of years old, and we don't understand any idea of what's going on, except in terms of the simplistic narrative wherein the little guy Zelensky is facing the tyrant Napoleon.

So, again, none of this justifies Putin's invasion, but consider what a person with a traditional Christian and Old World mindset like Putin's sees when he looks at Western culture today. When Putin sees the Soros puppet Zelensky performing his lewd acts on television and then becoming president of a country on his western border, it's not hard to understand why he believes that he must keep this rot from infecting his country. He has the same concerns I quoted Macron and Farage expressing in Chapter 3. And he knows that the degenerate cabal in control of American universities and government wants to undermine Russian culture just as it has undermined its own.

THE SEWER BOWL

Let me go back to the 2014 Super Bowl for an example of what I am talking about. I have nothing against any of the languages spoken on Earth. I just happen to prefer English spoken in America. But when I saw the multicultural, multilingual Coca-Cola Super Bowl ad, I wanted to smash my television with a brick. Coca-Cola should have fired anyone who came up with the idea for the ad. Better yet, those people should have been deported.

The commercial opened with "America the Beautiful," sung by a woman with a beautiful voice. There were images of a pickup truck, cowboys, and horses. It was very moving. Then, suddenly, the song was being sung in a different language. And then another language, and then another. It was in Hindi, Senegalese, and Arabic. As the language changed, so did the images. And instead of cowboys, you had women in burkas and two "dads" roller skating with their daughter.

It was the first Super Bowl ad to feature a homosexual family.[64] Let me explain why this ad was not patriotic. If you were to show a Coca-Cola ad in China that began with the Chinese national anthem in Mandarin and then suddenly broke into English and other languages, the Chinese would burn down the theater. If you're gay and have an adopted daughter and you want to roller skate, be my guest. I don't think it's right, but I'm not going to argue with you about it. But I do care when Coca-Cola makes you emblematic of the nation that I love. You're not emblematic. Look what the demented left has done to Budweiser, Target, and all the other once-dominant American brands by forcing the LGBTQ+ agendas down our throats!

I'm an American, and I'm sick and tired of having to make excuses for the United States. This has gone on too long on every level. People must stop debasing our most cherished possession, our pride in our nation. The reason that Coca-Cola was able to get away with that commercial and that ad companies are able to get away with ads in which there are almost no white people anymore is that we now live in a nation whose moral fiber has degenerated in the media. The Biden administration's relentless assault on our borders, language, and culture has expanded to include an assault on every one of our fundamental values and institutions, including family values.

This administration is out to destroy a once righteous and heroic America and replace it with a leftist government defined by immorality and greed. Biden's immigrant surge threatens to destroy America itself.

It's obvious what our nation is becoming with regard to language. You have illiterate morons who can't speak more than 50 words of English rubbing their crotches and being held up as role models. There are illegals coming in who are illiterate or hardly literate in *their own languages*. What are they doing to our culture? Are we becoming cultural Marxists?

Well, as I see it, in addition to doing everything it can to eliminate our borders, the Biden administration is promoting a stealth takeover of our government, our educational system, our popular culture, and journalism in this country. The advance of leftist values and policies that characterize this takeover has weakened the moral and cultural foundations on which this country rose to become the most powerful nation on Earth.

Under the Biden administration, the war on culture has expanded to include the left's war on Christians, on women, on men, on children, on minorities, and even on the rule of law. What most people don't understand is that this war has been waged by liberal leadership for well over a century, dating back to the Civil War.

STEM STUPIDITY

Our once-great universities are being turned into swamps. They have admitted people who could never keep up academically with anybody on the basis of color, sexual orientation, anything except academic standards. As a result, they have polluted virtually everything they have touched.

I received an email from a friend at San Diego State University. Apparently, there is a new category of professor. It's called a "Professor of Identity and Justice in STEM Education" at the University of Missouri, Columbia. Now STEM stands for "science, technology, engineering, and math"—and idiot. A total and absolute Marxist idiot has been allowed into this university in a department that's supposed to teach science, technology, engineering, and math with the title "Assistant Professor of Identity and Justice in STEM Education."

And so I received another email from a woman at San Diego State University, and she said: "You're invited to a conversation on power, structural racism and perceptions of normality in STEM through a lens of critical race theory with Dr. Tyrrell Morton, Assistant Professor of Identity and Justice in STEM Education at the University of Missouri, Columbia."

The email says that a so-called Dr. Martin will provide participants with professional development in equity and justice through
naming systemic racism and unpacking its implications on the lived
experience of racial minorities. Through this approach, informed
by critical race theory, participants will receive tangible tools and
resources that prompt awareness, understanding, and action toward
racial equity and justice through individual and personal as well as
individual professional roles and responsibilities. The email continues: "The webinar will consist of a lecture followed by an optional
interactive conversation in which participants will explore ways to
implement principles from the lecture. We invite you to attend the
lecture and participate in the conversation. This event is hosted by
the CSU Council on Ocean Affairs, Science and Technology."

I want to pause right here. The CSU Council on Ocean Affairs,
Science and Technology has installed a racist to teach a course on
racism and perceptions of normality in a program that's supposed
to be teaching students about science, technology, engineering, and
math. Can you believe what I am quoting to you? A group that is
supposed to be teaching on marine and coastal-related activities has
brought in a deviant Marxist to teach a course on racism, meaning
teaching racism against white people and against normal, heterosexual people. I and many others have been warning you for years
about the "Long March" through the universities. Now I've given
you another example. And as I said to you earlier, this began well
over a century ago, dating back to the Civil War.

The email I just referenced is the result of this century and a half
of moral erosion. The universities have been poisoned, polluted.
You cannot turn on a TV or open a website, you can't open a newspaper (those that exist) or a magazine without being bombarded

with filth that would have gotten its creators jailed little more than a half-century ago.

The degenerate leftists and their lack of principles are behind the disappearance of moral and cultural decency that has overtaken our federal government and many of our most important institutions, from the Department of Justice to the IRS to the U.S. military. Our institutions are rife with corruption that threatens our politics and national security.

The history of the political convictions that have consistently formed the foundation of the left's agenda is a history of anger at and hatred of religion, capitalism, individual initiative, and heterosexuality. Leftists hate the very foundations of Western culture. Every baseless critique launched by contemporary Democrats brands them as implicitly remorseless and unapologetic practitioners of a reductive and degenerate method of operation based on lies and unrelenting criticism of the opposition.

The leftist commitment to destroying capitalism and democratic government itself has metastasized to the point where we no longer have an option. We've got to find ways to eliminate the influence they've accumulated as they infiltrate every aspect of American life. What we're facing in the United States today is the dominance of cultural Marxism.

SUPREME SUICIDE

Ketanji Brown Jackson seems like a kindhearted person, the kind of person you would want as a neighbor, and it's important to see the positive in people before we go into the negative. She was nominated to replace the most radical left-wing ACLU justice known to mankind, Ruth Bader Ginsburg, who wreaked havoc on the police, the family, schools, and law enforcement for decades.

Jackson looks like a harmless, nice person, but in fact, to me, her rulings on child pornography and other issues make her as dangerous as Maxine Waters, Nancy Pelosi, Sheila Jackson Lee, and "The Squad" combined. Moreover, nothing distinguishes her in her rulings and sparse writings. She is not in the top category of intellects that we have seen on the Supreme Court. She is not an Oliver Wendell Holmes, a Louis Brandeis, or an Earl Warren. These were liberal justices, but they were giants intellectually who could move audiences with their rhetoric, their language, and their findings. We need someone who can elevate the Court, not make it sound as though it's just a municipal night court somewhere fixing traffic tickets.

Jackson was asked by Senator Ted Cruz if critical race theory is taught in schools, specifically kindergarten through twelfth grade. She replied, "Senator, I don't know, I don't think so. I believe it's an academic theory that's at the law school level."[65] The problem with that answer is that Jackson serves on the board of trustees for the Georgetown Day School, which Cruz then showed included in its curriculum books titled, *Critical Race Theory: An Introduction*, *The End of Policing: An Advocacy for Abolishing Police*, and *How to Be an Anti-Racist*.[66]

This is why I say she is not merely unimpressive, she's dangerous. These aren't necessarily unrelated traits. It is her uncritical acceptance of far-left concepts that makes her so dangerous.

When I looked up her record on sex offenses, I was similarly very worried about this very nice young woman because she said regarding some child pornography offenders, "I'm wondering whether you could say that there could be a less-serious child pornography offender, who is engaging in the type of conduct in the group experience level, because their motivation is the challenge or to use the technology. They're very sophisticated technologically, but they aren't necessarily that interested in the child pornography piece of it."[67]

I couldn't believe what I was hearing. She is soft on child pornography, just like Ruth Bader Ginsburg. This is exactly a repeat of history all over again, but even worse because again she doesn't have an independent mind. She's malleable, and she's just basically parroting what the far left wants her to say.

This is why, when asked by Senator Marsha Blackburn to provide a definition of the word "woman," Jackson was unable even to do that. "No, I can't. . . . Not in this context. I'm not a biologist."[68]

Do you see what I mean about the rot in American universities? The whole world is watching this country self-destruct—our allies, our rivals, and our enemies. Ketanji Brown Jackson is a perfect example of what American universities are turning out, based on teaching climate change, critical race theory, transgenderism, and the rest of the woke canon while denigrating classic literature, history, and hard science.

The Democrats have done a lot better than her. They could have found an African American woman who is liberal, who is far more literate, far more knowledgeable, and far more oriented toward America's values. But they did not want to. They wanted someone who can't give you a definition of the word "woman" on the highest court in the land. This is how cultural degeneration becomes codified into law and into the Constitution.

"TRANSANITY" IN SPORTS

One of the stranger depravations of our culture is trans women athletes. We all know this is insanity. The part of it that's most insane is not that a man identifies as a woman. That's been going on since the beginning of time. What is insane is to say that a man can compete as a woman when he is a man. This totally upsets the whole balance of the sexes.

The current teachings of gender or sex is total insanity. You can argue almost anything today. It's so relative to your orientation. In America, the criminal is now the victim. The cop is now the perpetrator of crime. So everything has been turned upside down by the vermin in the media and, of course, the communists who have taken control of the language. Therefore, if you want to be a woman, even though you're a man, you can say you're a woman, and that's your business, I suppose.

Transgender people are dangerous in sports because men are biologically different from women. This is a fact of reality that has been known forever. Let me tell you about a great gal named "Lucy." Lucy is a collection of fossilized skeletal remains of one of the oldest known human ancestors, *Australopithecus afarensis*. Her remains were discovered in 1974 at Hadar, Ethiopia, by paleoanthropologist Donald Johanson of the Cleveland Museum of Natural History.[69]

Lucy is believed to have lived 3.2 million years ago. What does this have to do with transgender athletes? Well, only this: Johanson knew immediately that the skeleton found was female. How? Because of her flared pelvis and wide pelvic opening. The flare gives more surface area from muscles that support a pregnant belly, and the larger opening allows for the birth of babies with larger brains.

Johanson's judgment has since been confirmed by DNA testing. It shows us that females in the human ancestral line have had a distinct skeletal structure for more than three million years. That's until now, of course. We're no longer supposed to acknowledge what real science teaches us.

This physiologic difference has great consequence for sports activity, with the hips spaced more widely apart. The thigh bone meets the knee at a knock-kneed angle that is not as straight up and down as a male's thigh bone. This is a less efficient weight-bearing structure and leads to more injuries, such as anterior cruciate ligament (ACL) tendon tears, which are more frequent in female soccer players than in males.

This is a scientific fact. You can't change science to match your desires, even though this insanity is sweeping the globe. While not as obvious as size and strength, this structural difference between genetic males and genetic females can be extremely significant in rough contact sports.

World Rugby recently released new guidelines that ban transgender women from playing the sport with other women due to "player welfare risks."[70] The updated regulations, according to NBC, are "among the most exclusionary policies for transgender athletes instituted by an international federation to date, and they're a departure from major governing bodies' policies on trans inclusion, including the International Olympic Committee's rules that permit trans women to compete in the Olympics provided they maintain a certain testosterone level for 12 months prior to competition."[71]

Some countries have rejected this ban on transgender women in rugby. Unsurprisingly, they include the United States, England, Canada, New Zealand, and France—nations whose cultures are collapsing. They value *inclusion* over reality.

So you can have it any way you want, but you can't argue with biology. I know that this is considered anathema today. But that's the way it is. It's all a question of whether you believe in biology, history, and anthropology or you merely believe in what you want to feel. This all started with, "If it feels good, do it." It ended with insanity.

Prior to the 2022 Beijing Winter Olympics, the International Olympic Committee (IOC) put out a six-page set of guidelines called,

"IOC Framework on Fairness, Inclusion and Non-Discrimination on the Basis of Gender Identity and Sex Variations." This is how insane your world has become, because the smallest minority of mentally unstable people has taken over every aspect of culture, including the Olympics.

This so-called framework instructs organizers, organizations, and athletes that "everyone, regardless of their gender identity, expression and/or sex variations, should be able to participate in sport safely and without prejudice."[72] The NCAA issued a similar statement. The introduction to the document states: "Every person has the right to practice sport without discrimination and in a way that respects their health, safety, and dignity. At the same time, the credibility of competitive sport—and particularly high-level organized sporting competitions—relies on a level playing field, where no athlete has an unfair and disproportionate advantage over the rest."[73]

This is nonsense in plain English. Owing to differences in bone physiology, safe and fair competition on a level playing field becomes almost or totally impossible when women athletes compete against women athletes who are transitioning from male.

I had the opportunity to interview an expert on bone density, John Jaquish, PhD, from Rushmore University. He said that bone size and density can play a major role in the outcome of all sports, especially contact sports. Many severe fractures have occurred in contact sports—the potential for injury is greater if trans women are allowed to compete against biological women.

Here is one question I've been asking since this insanity began: Where are the women's groups? Where are all the people who stand up for women saying that this is totally insane, that matching women athletes with trans women who are really men is resulting in life-threatening injuries? These injuries are due to larger, denser bones impacting against thinner, less-dense bones in the skull, neck, and spine of the women. This is what happens when left-wing fanatics get control of a society.

HIPPIE MARXISTS

In the 1960s, the slogan was "Make love, not war." That became the rallying cry of a generation of hippies and leftist subversives who opposed the war in Vietnam. These words were credited to Herbert Marcuse, a communist professor who escaped Nazi Germany in the 1930s and set up shop in America. Marcuse and another popular Marxist author, Eric Fromm, became influential leaders in the movement toward Marxism in this country.

Both Marcuse and Fromm were proponents of what was called "polymorphic sexuality." This term represented for them the ultimate liberation of mankind from sexual repression and the need to work for a living. They envisioned a society in which American citizens would give up individual freedom to the state and become pleasure-seeking functionaries whose only value consisted of pushing the envelope of hedonism.

You can open up virtually any website and see how far this has been ramped up and how degenerate this nation has become. With regard to the meltdown of the moral foundations of this nation, Marxist culture is being imposed on the most vulnerable of Americans, our children. It's invaded everything from our military to the Christian churches and communities so reviled by the left. Many of the Christian churches now are Marxist churches.

As I've said many times on my radio show and podcast over many years, I'm a sexual libertarian. What you want to do with a consenting partner is your business. I don't care. You could dress up like Tinker Bell and run around your bedroom in tights and a tutu. As long as

I don't have to watch you, I don't care. I should say that I don't care as long as it's within the law, you're not hurting another person, and it doesn't involve children—*and as long as you don't run the country.*

But take a look at what's around Biden. Take a look at what's running this country now. Marxist culture, you see, is built on the inherent distrust of strong males. The cultural Marxists have their hatred of men and their suppression of maleness based on the fact that they see patriarchal societies and culture as the enemies of the state. This is why so many militant lesbians have declared themselves Marxists, such as the two militant lesbian con women who run Black Lives Matter.

Male-dominated capitalism equals oppression to these Communists, or so they say. They beat this drum to rally those who feel oppressed. A virile, successful man is cast as the enemy, whether black, white, Hispanic, or Asian. The left's agenda can succeed only if the male population is neutralized, and this empowered part of this administration's war against American males is carried out through what I see as its decimation of military leadership.

This country is in dire straits. I used to say, not entirely facetiously, that America's future hangs in the balance like a loose tooth. I said that while Obama was decimating this country—attacking the police, attacking white people, attacking the middle class, all the while laughing all the way to the bank with his wife, Michelle.

CHAPTER 6

THE BANKRUPTCY PLOT

The difference between a conservationist and an
environmentalist is the former employs reason,
while the latter is nothing more than a religious fanatic.
And I don't mean a deeply religious person in a rational
way. I mean a snake handler who doesn't mind committing
suicide in the false belief that God will be pleased.

B Y THE TIME YOU read this, President Biden hopes that you firmly believe that the outrageous inflation you're suffering is all Vladimir Putin's fault. He wants you to forget that inflation was 7 percent in 2021, the highest it had been since 1982.[74] Putin didn't invade Ukraine until February 2022. Not even a liberal could believe that Putin could make prices go up in the past.

When Donald Trump left office, inflation was at 1.4 percent.[75] Biden managed to increase it 500 percent in one year. Impressive, in a horrible way!

Of course, it's not just economics. It's the emotional toll that Biden and his gang are placing on the American people. We can go down the list, but this administration seems to be living and stuck in the 1960s. It's as if Rip Van Winkle has met Frankenstein and Neville Chamberlain all rolled into one.

So, I'm going to call him Rip Van Biden. The emotional and mental burden this administration had placed on the public is devastating. They are trying to destroy the constitutional republic on a daily basis, taking it apart at the joints. They're sweeping the crime wave under the rug and ramping up constant hatred against white people, and the military's witch hunt for extremists. But those are almost collateral issues.

"BIDENFLATION"

Remember, they used COVID-19 to get rid of Trump. They said that he was responsible for it. They said that he didn't do the right thing. They said that he didn't do this, didn't do that. Well, after Biden took over, there were no home test kits even after Biden had a chance to buy them months before. Then came his attempt to impose vaccine mandates, which angered tens of millions of people. That all contributed to the misery index as well.

But the main contributor to American misery has been stagflation. I'm sure you're very familiar with that term, raging inflation in the midst of a stagnant economy. So how do we know when we've reached stagflation, and how close are we to bridging the gap?

Well, I was paying $6.46 a gallon for gas at the time of this writing. So I will tell you that we have stagflation when I fill up my tank and it costs me $100. It's as simple as that. But for the average person, it's the price of eggs, milk, and vegetables. Average people know it at the supermarket. They know it in their pocketbooks. And by the way, Americans vote with their pocketbooks, so they don't have to know what words like "stagflation" or "inflation" mean. All they have to know is that when they go to buy eggs, the eggs cost 50 percent more than they did a year ago. Or when gas costs 30, 40, or 50 percent more. They would say that this is no good. And all they know is that there's less money to go around—and they're going to blame Biden, as they should.

Now very high inflation isn't stagflation unless it's accompanied by high unemployment. This is the combination Keynesians always said was impossible. The 1970s stagflation settled that matter, but somehow Keynesians still run everything. Well, if you believe unemployment is really low today, then there is no stagflation.

The Federal Reserve began raising interest rates in March 2022 when it finally realized that inflation wasn't "transitory." As usual, the Fed was the last to know where the economy was headed. It's always reluctant to raise interest rates because Wall Street doesn't like it. So, by the time the Fed started raising rates, the horses had left the barn.

I have news for Federal Reserve Chairman Jay Powell. I lived through Jimmy Carter's reign of incompetence, and Main Street doesn't actually mind higher interest rates because people put their money into the banks and make a lot of interest. We were making 15 percent interest on our money in banks under Jimmy Carter. People thought it was great.

When interest rates were artificially low, house prices went through the ceiling, and people who own property were thrilled because their houses were worth more than they paid for them, especially in California. You can't even find a house to buy in my home state. So, we come back to interest rates. When the Fed raises interest rates, which is very important in controlling the value of the dollar, it slows the economy, which is necessary, according to leading economists, to prevent massive inflation, leading to a Weimar Republic–like meltdown of our currency.

So, once inflation was out of control, every economist was screaming for the Fed to raise interest rates, knowing that it would lead to an economic downturn. But I remind you that this cycle was started with the 500 percent increase in the inflation rate during 2021 and exacerbated by Biden's sanctions on Russia, which hurt Americans as much as they did Russians and Vladimir Putin not at all.

BILLIONAIRE BAILOUTS

Credit Suisse is a Swiss bank that has been around for 167 years but could not survive two years of Biden's shenanigans. Here in the United States, Silicon Valley Bank (SVB) similarly went up in flames. None of the big depositors were insured, and yet they bailed them out and said it's not a bailout. What was it, then? Yale senior economics fellow at the Brookings Institution, Aaron Klein, said that's what it is, plain and simple.[76] Brookings is a liberal think tank, by the way.

Klein spent more than 10 ten years working in government, including his time as chief economist of the Senate Banking, Housing, and Urban Affairs Committee. And during the time that Klein worked in the government, he worked on the Troubled Asset Relief Program, which was a $700 billion government bailout authorized by Congress in October of 2008. He knows a bailout when he sees one.

The depositors being made whole on their deposits in the bank, beyond the $250,000 FDIC guarantee, are getting bailed out. Anyone with deposits less than that were already guaranteed their money back without this action by the Fed. But the question is: Who was bailed out in the SVB disaster? In plain English, it was big Democrat loud-mouthed donors, even though it was illegal to do so.

Moving money around like this and bailing out your friends and donors is a bigger crime than paying off a hooker. Just after the bank collapsed, actress Sharon Stone said, "I just lost half my money to this banking thing [presumably referring to the SVB collapse]."[77] Investor Kevin O'Leary, who had a huge amount of money at the failed bank, said the institution was "run by idiots."[78] To his credit, O'Leary criticized the bailout even though he benefited from it. He said, in so many words, that no bank will bother to be responsible going forward because they know the Federal Reserve will bail them out if they get in similar trouble.[79]

Peter Thiel, a very smart man, said that he had $50 million of his own money stuck in SVB when it shut down.[80] But he didn't lose that $50 million. Biden gave it back to him. Out of my back pocket and yours, even if only indirectly through the effects of inflation. California Governor Gavin Newsom was a client of SVB. He had personal accounts at the bank for years, and his three businesses had their accounts at the SVB. He didn't mention that when he praised the bailout publicly.[81]

As I said, they aren't taking the money to bail out these million-aires and billionaires directly out of our bank accounts. They are creating it out of thin air. When you keep printing money, you're going to put upward pressure on prices. Everyone seems to know that from Economics 101 in college except Joe Biden and Janet "the Yenta" Yellen.

Apparently, Yellen never passed Economics 101, but she's the head of the Treasury Department. She doesn't know the first thing about money, but she's running the Treasury Department. How could they put a yenta like that in such a crucial position? Only under Biden.

This is why I supported Jerome Powell's decision to keep raising rates. Otherwise, gasoline will eventually be over $10 a gallon. Bread will be $8 a loaf. I suppose they will still blame Donald Trump for that, even though we didn't see inflation until Biden got in there.

THE CHINESE AUCTION ON AMERICAN FARMLAND

Should America reclaim all U.S. farms owned by China? I've been asking this question for years as the Chinese have been cleverly buying up our mines, our farms, our ports, the very air we breathe. I don't blame the Chinese government for this. I blame the political class, Democrat and Republican, because never forget how many Republicans went to work as lobbyists for China.

Democrat Madeleine "Half-Price" Albright was one of the worst of all of them, one of the lowest of human beings. To be fair, though, on the Republican side there was also the war hero from World War II, Bob Dole. Dole himself became a lobbyist for China.[82] I suppose a man's gotta make a buck.

After all, there were people who sold trucks to Hitler before World War II. In fact, Henry Ford put a Ford plant in Germany before the war to build trucks for Hitler. Did that make Henry Ford a crypto-Nazi? Not really. He was just a businessman looking out for his business, which means that you can't let businessmen dictate government policy in every case. Sometimes the people have to dictate policy, and I am saying that it's time to take back all the U.S. farms owned by China.

It was also a Republican, George W. Bush, who tried to give security for six of our national ports of entry to Dubai.[83] I raised a national outcry about it. I should have won a prize for it, but I don't need a prize. The prize was stopping them. That was prize enough, and it was Michael Savage, not Chuck Schumer, who pushed against the Dubai ports deal with the help of my enormous audience. The outcry we raised through my radio show, "The Savage Nation," stopped George Bush from transferring the security of six of our national ports to Dubai.

If you remember the case, it was enormous, and strangely enough, one of the most prominent members of Congress agreed with me at the time. That was Chuck Schumer. I had him on my show in February 2006—politics makes strange bedfellows indeed.

And together, as Americans, we put our national interest ahead of our political interests and said no to George Bush. We said no to Dubai taking over our ports, and we stopped them from taking over port security.

Who will stop China now? It already owns so much of our farmland. China owns our pork production, cattle production, wheat production, and soybean production. They almost own our minds. God knows what else has been given away.

Note that I am not suggesting that we seize the land from its Chinese owners. I said *reclaim*. Reclaiming it means instead of bailing out Catholic churches, the government could bail out the Chinese and just give them back the money or take it out of some other fund. I don't care. Just pay them off and take back the farmlands.

It's time to tell the Chinese that they can't own the very land that we use for our food production. That's stupid. I can think of a harsher, more accurate term than *stupid*, but I'll leave it at that.

I enjoy the television show, *My Brilliant Friend*, on HBO. It's a small show in a way, but fabulous. It's about postwar Italy and the poverty and the poor people. It traces the lives of two women starting out as young girls in this little housing project outside of Naples. And the story is told covering a period of seven years in the lives of the two women—the boyfriends, the marriages, the divorces, the children.

The show really struck me because I grew up in America in a lower-middle-class home. I wouldn't say poor because we weren't impoverished, but we were, I would say, at the lower end of the lower middle class. We were an immigrant family and didn't complain about it. I had three meals a day and all that.

I talked about this show in a podcast titled, "A Peasant's View of the World," back in 2020 because the life that I led as a child was very much like the lives of the children that I saw in that show. Why did I choose that title? Well, I said I have kept my mind clutter free of the trappings of my success. Let me put it to you this way: I do not let the trappings of my own success clutter my thinking, and I try to continue to think as I would have as a poor man—not because it's noble, but because it keeps my mind clear.

And so, I talked about what we were living through in 2020 under the dictatorship of the governors—under the dictatorship of these nameless, faceless feminist bureaucrats who stole our freedom and used the police as their Gestapo to beat people up who didn't wear a mask. I talked about how American business will look after this all-out attack on it. I said, "We've seen the flash, we've heard the bomb go off, but we have not yet seen the devastation."

We haven't seen the end of it even now. President Biden wants you to think that the food shortages he announced are all because of Putin, but they're not. In 2020, we saw farmers pouring out milk into streams.[84] They destroyed their own crops.[85] They culled livestock.[86] The food shortages are the result of governmental misman-agement of agricultural policy. And you could blame any side you want. I really don't care. Government mismanagement of agricul-tural policy is responsible for this insanity.

As a child, I was told to finish my plate, and if I didn't finish my plate, my mother put it in the refrigerator and reheated it the next day. Why? Because we were told not to waste food. It's another time and another place. But I'm afraid when I tell you this that many of us are going to have to learn how to think like peasants in order to survive in the future.

So foreign ownership of our farmland is very worrisome to me. And China not only owns our livestock production in many cases but our farmland as well. Do you know that China purchased Syngenta, a pesticides and seed company. Do you know that Syngenta owns the seeds that farmers use to plant our crops?

But when you realize that there's going to be food shortages to begin with and then you realize that the communist Chinese own our supply of various farm products and the land itself, there's going to be a time when this pebble I'm throwing into this pond of thought will create the ripples that will reach you.

Now let me start with which states have the most foreign ownership. Would you believe that Texas is the number one state that has sold itself to foreign entities? Old Maine, which used to be a Republican stronghold, is number two.[87]

Alabama, Washington state, and Michigan round out the top five. But here's the kicker: Six states have laws banning foreign ownership of farmland.[88] Those states are Hawaii, Iowa, Minnesota, Mississippi, North Dakota, and Oklahoma. It's a short list. Six states at some point had the brains, the wisdom, the patriotism, the sanity, the survivability to say that foreigners cannot own their farmland.

In the year of 2013, one week before the Chinese company Qinghai purchased Smithfield Foods, the largest producer of pork products in the world, the Missouri legislature amended a law clearing the way for the acquisition.[89] In other words, the Chinese lobbied the Missouri legislature and said we want China to buy Smithfield Foods and we want you to make it happen.

Now, before that, Missouri had a law on its books that banned all foreign ownership of farmland. But that bill then raised the ceiling to 1 percent ownership, saying, okay, well, we'll let foreigners own 1 percent. That little move allowed the company that was once known as Smithfield, now known as WH Group, to acquire more than 40,000 acres of Missouri farmland, according to federal data.

This was a very big story. Maybe not big to you today because it's not in the news, but because the president of the United States has now told the American people that there are going to be food shortages in this country, I thought I would remind you who is in control of some of the farmland where what food you get will be grown. Maybe this is a good time to answer my question on whether we should take it back.

ELECTRIC VIRTUE VEHICLES

Long before Joe Biden crippled the U.S. economy with sanctions on Russia for the invasion he helped provoke, the Democrats were assaulting the economy with their war on fossil fuels. Believing in their flawed global warming theory like a religion, no cost to American citizens is too high in the worship of their Earth goddess, Gaia.

They don't care if you lose heating energy in the middle of winter.[90] They don't care if you can't afford meat or other protein-rich alternatives. "Eat bugs, peasant," they tell you.[91] And they don't care if you can't afford to drive to work. "Take the bus," they say,[92] while they fly around the world to their climate conferences in private jets.

Their other answer is for everyone to buy electric vehicles. Never mind that most people can't afford to pay for their internal combustion engine cars without a long-term loan. Like I said, the peasants can take the bus, as far as they're concerned. But for all those who can just manage to make payments on these supposedly "green" vehicles, they want them to be forced to buy them.

All of this is based on the assumption that electric vehicles really are "greener." I have news for you. They're not.

When considering electric vehicles, you have to begin at the beginning. The beginning is the first law of thermodynamics, which states that energy cannot be created or destroyed. This is a very important concept when we talk about electric cars. In other words, you can't get something for nothing. The total quantity of energy in the universe stays the same. So what does this have to do with electric cars? What does this have to do with "blood batteries"? What does this have to do with the real cost of electric vehicles?

Let me begin by saying that I am fundamentally a conservationist. I'm an animal rights activist. We fund animal groups. We take care of animals the best we can. Believe me, I have been involved in environmental causes or conservation causes since I was a teenager.

It's important that you understand that I would have liked clean energy from the beginning of time, when the early humans first discovered that they could put two pieces of wood under their feet and ski down a hill. They thought that they could get energy for nothing. Then they realized that they had to trudge up that hill to go down the hill on those two pieces of wood called skis.

When mankind first set out from the shores in their little canoes or rowboats, they realized that it would be nice if they didn't have to row across large expanses of water. And then they discovered the sail. That was wonderful. But, of course, that wind energy was not created, it was not destroyed, it was just used.

When it comes to electric vehicles, the batteries that you are using in your car or other electric vehicle cost an awful lot of energy to manufacture. Great environmental costs are involved in creating batteries. You may not want to hear this, all you good liberals out there, but child labor in the Congo in Africa accounts for up to

30 percent of Congo's cobalt.[93] The country of Congo mines more than 70 percent of the global total of cobalt.

Children are forced to work in those mines—African children, black children, the ones good white liberals pretend to care so much about. Liberals think electric vehicles are cleaner, better, and finer than anything else because they don't emit any carbon. But what about the total fuel consumption for the mining of cobalt and the manufacture of electric car batteries? Doesn't that cost something?

Biden is pushing electric vehicles. Elon Musk is the richest man on Earth. It's hard to believe that the original electric car, the "lowly" Prius, has been with us for 20 years. The Prius, with its humble profile and free pass to California's carpool lanes these days, the once celebrated Prius, now seems a little clunky and outmoded, doesn't it?

Along has come Elon Musk and Tesla—sleeker, sexier, more muscular. The Prius, a hybrid, went from 0 to 60 in about 10.3 seconds. Tesla does it in about 2.5 seconds, and it's all electric, not just partly electric.[94] In contrast, every new technology brings risks, especially if the technology is pushed too fast. Teslas have been known to blow up unexpectedly on freeways.[95] The self-driving version does sometimes take a wrong turn.[96]

Self-driving electric cars also emit radiation.[97] They're like gigantic microwave ovens that emit radiation that may be very harmful to humans. Now, these concerns don't get as much attention from the media as Musk's ventures into space, but those can blow up as well.[98]

The fact that Democrats are full steam ahead on the Green New Deal and electric car promotion tells us that when technology is made ruler over everything, as we've seen recently with social media technology and what it has done, having been permitted to go too fast, a little disaster here or there is considered nothing to worry about. Musk became the richest man on the planet in early January

2021, overtaking Jeff Bezos (but Bezos reclaimed the prize on February 16).

Why are the Democrats promoting all-electric-vehicle policy plans, and who stands to gain from them? Well, the Biden administration is proposing an all-electric requirement for federal government vehicles.[99] Many state and local governments will likely follow suit. Do you think that mandates for average Americans can be far behind? They mandated vaccines. Why shouldn't they mandate electric vehicles?

And yet, as with so many things in public policy—think of the COVID-19 responses—there is more hype and hysteria behind the electric car push than reason and logic. The hype comes from those in government and industry who stand to make fortunes from this conversion from gas to electric. The government–media complex, which operates hand in glove with Chinese business interests, includes Biden, McConnell, Feinstein, and God knows who else. We all know that China stands to profit enormously from a gas-to-electric conversion.

The hysteria comes from the wailing of climate alarmists, from that stupid girl Greta Thunberg in Europe to Hollywood hypocrites who take private jets. If you want some reason and logic with your morning coffee or your evening wine, I'm here to tell you that there's a lot more to the electric vehicle story than what you're being told. They may hold great promise, but today I will let you in on a dirty little secret. As it stands today, the electric car industry is not as environmentally clean as it would like you to believe, and it certainly isn't morally clean either.

In the "virtuous" mad dash to electrify every mode of transportation, no one seems to wonder if the plants that make the batteries for these vehicles create more pollution than the vehicles eliminate.

Well, it turns out they do. According to an article in *Auto Week*, "battery production for electric cars ultimately produces more carbon dioxide—up to 74 percent more—than an efficient conventional car if those batteries are produced in a factory powered by fossil fuels."[100]

If those batteries are produced in a factory powered by fossil fuels, as battery production scales up so will emissions from those factories—factories that themselves rely on less than clean energy to create the batteries. Henrik Fisker, CEO of Fisker, Inc., an American electric vehicle company, told Bloomberg: "It will come down to where is the battery made? How is it made and even where do we get our electric power from?"[101]

Another problem with producing these ion batteries is obtaining the materials. The metals needed are only mined in a few countries, like your friend, China. And once you've ignored that problem, you can go on to ignoring the question of where we get the energy needed to build the batteries. Did you think about that? Liberals don't care about these questions as long as they can feel greener than thou.

All the smug people at first in their Priuses thought they were better than you, and they would cut you off from the right lane while giving you the finger because of that false sense of superiority. But you can see that smugness is based on ignoring quite a few questions about electric vehicles that liberals never think to ask. I'll give you one more: Where does the energy to charge the electric vehicle come from? I have news for you, if the answer isn't a windmill farm, solar panels, or a nuclear plant, then you're burning fossil fuels to generate the electricity to charge the vehicle.

In other words, you pull up all smug in your little electric car to a charging station somewhere, a supermarket or outside a Macy's store, and you think that you're just a wonderful person who is "saving the planet." But did you ask yourself, where does the electricity come from? Well, it comes from somewhere. As I told you, you cannot create or destroy energy. It comes from something. For the most part, especially once electric vehicles are widely used, the electricity to charge them will come from burning fossil fuels. It doesn't matter if the electric car you're driving is not polluting while being driven and you feel clean as the driven snow, because the pollution to make the electricity was already released by the power plant where the electricity was generated. But as long as it's not in your back seat, you don't care.

So, if you're driving an electric car in the United States, you'll probably release more carbon dioxide into the atmosphere than if you're driving it in Iceland, which runs almost entirely on hydro, geothermal, and solar energy. But as long as it's not in your back seat, why care about it, right?

And now we have to look at the high cost of recycling lithium-ion batteries from electric vehicles. The cost to recycle these batteries is another of those hidden costs that no one ever talks about. Nice clean car.

There's a great article on this on Nature.com. They write: "Making conservative assumptions of an average battery pack weight of 250 kg and volume of half a cubic metre, the resultant pack wastes would comprise around 250,000 tonnes and half a million cubic metres of unprocessed pack waste, when these vehicles reach the end of their lives."[102] They go on to say that although reuse and current recycling processes can mitigate some of this, the burden of electric vehicle waste is still very substantial when you consider how many more of these vehicles Biden and the corrupt corporations want to push onto the American public.

You also have to figure out how to store the spent batteries until they are either recycled or disposed of. Recycling them requires a tremendous amount of chemical separation. So there is a lot to think about just in terms of what to do with the spent batteries.

The Nature.com article goes on to say: "A fire in stockpiled tyres in Powys, Wales, for example, smouldered for fifteen years from 1989 to 2004. Since the electrode materials in LIBs [lithium-ion batteries] are far more reactive than tyre rubber, without a proactive and economically sound waste-management strategy for LIBs, there are potentially greater dangers associated with stockpiling of end-of-life LIBs."[103]

So, there's a very, very high environmental cost of recycling lithium-ion batteries for electric vehicles. And I think you have to think about that the next time you want to buy one. What's the overall cost in terms of energy?

Biden says that his plan will save billions of gallons of oil and help create one million auto industry jobs by banning the sale or manufacture of new internal combustion engine vehicles by 2030. If you can't afford an electric vehicle, you can take the bus, as far as the great friend of the working man is concerned.

Exactly how this will happen in the real world he didn't say because it's total BS—it's all a lie. Following the lead of totalitarian China, U.S. automakers, not just Tesla, are all aboard for this big switchover. As I see it, internal combustion engine vehicles will be replaced, and gasoline stations will be transformed into electric vehicle charging stations. The pressure will be on to get rid of the remaining internal combustion engine vehicles and buy more electric vehicles. China-friendly General Motors plans to spend $20 billion on self-driving vehicle technology through 2025, including producing 23 different models of electric vehicles. Ford Motor Company has pledged to invest $11 billion in electric vehicle development.

Another downside of vastly increasing the number of electric vehicles is that the metals and minerals increasingly come from nations like China, Chile, and Congo, where fair wages, protections against child labor, workplace safety, and environmental standards are far below anything the United States or the European Union would tolerate. But that does not bother a liberal as long as it's not in their back seat. In fact, I could call this section "Not in My Back Seat" because they don't care that there are child slave laborers making the batteries for their clean, perfect little cars as long as it's not in their back seat. Electric vehicle batteries also require more energy to manufacture than batteries and engines for internal combustion vehicles, and recycling them is very complicated, expensive, and filled with pollution and public health risks down the road.

Someday, the human race will not be dependent on fossil fuels, and no one will be happier than me. I've been a conservationist for longer than most of Joe Biden's "enviro-Nazis" have been alive. The difference between a conservationist and an environmentalist is that the former employs reason, while the latter is nothing more than a religious fanatic. And I don't mean a deeply religious person in a rational way. I mean a snake handler who doesn't mind committing suicide in the false belief that God will be pleased.

The difference between them and the crazed liberals running our society is at least the snake handlers take their own risks. The mentally deranged elites in charge today want you to handle the snakes and take all the bites while they try to pretend it's saving the planet.

CHAPTER 7

THE CHAOS PLOT

Nobody wants to live in a city or a state
where liberal policies are actually implemented.

W E HAVE BECOME A third world nation of terror, riots, mobs, and chaos. This is also part of the plot. Biden is largely responsible for the chaos, the terror, the mobs, and the riots. He always seems to do the wrong thing. We have the horror going on in Ukraine, which is going to make Biden even more desperate to try and look like he's doing the right thing at home.

What does it mean when you have a mayor who calls white police officers "crackers" and still has his job?[104] When you have Joe Biden sitting in the Oval Office who used the race card while he was running for office? When you won't address the fundamental issue of a crime wave?

RE-FUND THE POLICE

In March 2022, Biden claimed, "I've said it before, the answer is not to defund our police departments, it's to fund our police and give them all the tools they need, training and foundation and partners and protectors that our communities need."[105] Did he say that before? I'm not so sure. When he was campaigning in 2020, he said police should be defunded and not defunded, sometimes during the same speech.[106] So I suppose he did say something like that before. He also said precisely the opposite. How do we know which one was the truth and which one a lie? Does Biden know?

The crime wave is multifactorial, by the way; it's not a single thing. Biden wants to blame the crime wave on guns. Guns don't shoot themselves. People use guns. So, if you want to talk about gun violence, I'm all for it. And if you want to round up guns, why don't you start with the gangs who have the guns?

You know, when I grew up in New York, if a cop got shot, which was extremely rare, the city shut down. There was no movement in the city. All the criminals stopped their activity until the person who shot that cop was arrested and given the death penalty. By the way, there were very few police attacked or shot in the 1950s when I was a child. And that is because we had tough-on-crime policies.

Not so today. You have George Soros, the maniac funding DAs who have made crime fashionable. He has made self-defense a crime. And you have flash mobs of thieves. That sounds very cool, doesn't it? It has become normalized in Manhattan for an upscale store to be broken into by these bums. How do you stop flash mobs? It's simple. Shoot the looters. I know that no one wants to hear this. Something drastic has to be done.

They beat up security guards. They beat up people in the stores. They are afraid of nobody because there are no consequences. So, Joe, we're all for supporting the police, but we're not for lip service. You were the one who attacked the thin blue line. And once you stripped the thin blue line away from cities, we got mobs. You have Black Lives Matter, and you have Antifa. They have names. They are organized.

DISARMING YOU
INSTEAD OF THE CRIMINALS

Of course, the mobs are not the people Biden wants to disarm. He believes that it will reduce crime to take guns away from people who don't break the law, people who might need their guns to defend themselves against those who do. In February 2022, Biden basically said so in one of his rambling tirades:

> There's no amendment that's absolute. When the amendment was passed, it didn't say anybody can own a gun, any kind of gun, and any kind of weapon. You couldn't buy a cannon when this amendment was passed, so there's no reason why you should be able to buy certain assault weapons.[107]

That's not even true, by the way. Even the left-wing PolitiFact was forced to debunk that one.[108] But we're not even arguing about owning cannons. Joe the Clown is trying to attack the Constitution. He wants to take guns away from law-abiding conservatives and leave them in the hands of the criminals, the mobs, and the anarchists.

I distinctly remember when the very liberal Supreme Court Justice Elena Kagan was being questioned during her confirmation hearings. She was very clear. She said that the Second Amendment is "settled law."[109] I have the tape recording in my head. She said that it's settled law. Joe Biden apparently missed that lesson when he went to Delaware State University or Amtrak University or wherever he went.

The fact of the matter is that it's not about guns; it's about the people who are illegally using guns. And there was a time when everyone in law enforcement knew who they were, and they would stop them and frisk them in the streets and take the guns away from them. New York had such a police division. They would stop people whom they knew or thought might be criminals and likely to be carrying guns, frisk them, take their guns away, lock them up in prison, and throw away the key. That all changed with the progressivism that has now infested and infected the nation.

The parole boards these days are printing "get out of jail free cards." One of the Sacramento mass-shooting suspects was in prison for a 10-year sentence for previous felony convictions. He was released by a psycho leftist parole board. The county even paid him $7,000 in damages for injuries from a gang attack in jail due to the supposed negligence of a guard.[110]

The Sacramento County Deputy District Attorney Danielle Abogado didn't want him released in the first place. In a letter to the parole board, she wrote: "He is an assaultive and noncompliant individual who has absolutely no regard for his victims, who are left in the wake of numerous serious offenses. If he is released early, he will continue to break the law."[111]

And the parole board let this maniac out anyway!

So, right away, the governor jumps in and says that we must restrict guns. I say no, restrict felons, meaning that it's illegal for a felon to possess a gun. I would say that if a felon uses a gun in a crime that results in death, a murder, the felon goes to jail for life. No parole. That would put a damper on it. That's the first thing.

Second, I think the clubs have to be closed earlier. What is a club, anyway? It's a hangout for the general drug culture of gun-toting psychopathic criminals. I say close at 11 o'clock. What's wrong with that? What kind of person goes to a club at 3 o'clock in the morning other than a bummer or a slacker? Who else has time to hang around in a club with a bunch of junkies and drugs and guns until just before sunrise but bad people?

Don't get me wrong. I did go to dance clubs when I was younger, but nobody had guns. We worked in the morning, so we had to go home at a certain time. The clubs have become dens of psychopathic behavior. Drugs are sold in clubs. Guns are transferred in clubs. Everything illegal happens in these so-called clubs. I would say that there has to be restrictions on clubs.

I don't know why anybody would be opposed to that. Why shouldn't they be closed earlier? Who would be harmed by this? Smiley Martin and his dear brother Dandrae? They didn't go to the club that late to do dance moves. They went there to shoot people, according to reports. The first one, Dandrae Martin, was also a convicted felon.[112] How did he get a gun? If a felon is caught using a gun that results in death, he should be given life in prison without parole.

Let's talk about the crime wave from the point of view of the breakdown of families. I study nature. If you watch a pack of lions, the mother lion teaches the baby lion what to do, and if that lion cub steps out of line, the mother nudges it or slaps it and puts it back in line because the cub will get killed if it steps out of line. The hyenas are waiting to eat it.

Now let's look at America today. In most black homes, no fathers, hardly any mothers. The children are growing up themselves. Never mind latchkey kids. They are raising themselves. They're watching MTV. They're watching violence on television. They're watching disgusting vermin performing rap music. They're listening to left-wing politicians telling them it's okay to do anything they want to do. That they are poor because of white privilege. Because of "systemic racism." As a result, mobs of teens attack and rob at will. We are becoming a New Zimbabwe.

This is the end result of liberalism. It's a death philosophy, and it has to end and has to end fast. It has to end with tough crime laws. It's a simple concept that we all understand. It's commonsense crime and punishment. You take away punishment, crime goes up; you increase punishment, crime goes down—whether it's a teacher in a schoolroom or a parent at home. Children need to be told what to do or they're wild animals. Everybody knows that they're not inherently knowledgeable about what to do. They have to be taught. And even adults need incentives—rewards for good behavior and punishment for bad behavior. I think everybody would agree with that.

For years, I've talked about the thin blue line being the only thing between us and total chaos. You probably remember that from 20 years ago. Everyone knows about the thin blue line. When you defund the police, call police officers every name under the sun, arrest them, and cut their budgets, you end up with these violent teens running wild in the streets.

ANARCHIST APPS

The criminals now have apps they use to plan their break-ins. In late 2021, some criminals broke into a Home Depot in southern California.[113] It was the Friday after Thanksgiving. And what did they steal, these upstanding citizens? The stole sledgehammers and bolt cutters so that they could break into more stores. How did they organize this mob of at least 10 lowlifes?

Well, anyone who has an iPhone has a system called an iMessage right on the phone. There are other apps such as Signal Wire and Telegram that permit bad people to set up illicit gatherings. You could say that they just use it for parties. Then why do they need it to disappear in three minutes?

These apps are used by drug dealers, prostitution rings, child traffickers, and animals like this. And so, if they're using these apps, I want to know why Tim Cook is not allowing the FBI to break into these iPhones to catch these people.

Do you remember a few years ago when two Muslims went to work on a crowd of coworkers and killed them?[114] For weeks, there was an argument between Apple, meaning Tim Cook, and the FBI trying to get into the iPhones of one of the perpetrators of that massacre. And Tim Cook wouldn't yield. He said that he believes in privacy.[115] Are you joking?

It's all about the bottom line. It has nothing to do with privacy. And we have to come to understand that this country cannot sustain such a crime wave. We all have to agree that without order, there is no social order, and without social order, there is no society. It's crumbling here in California, where San Francisco has been hollowed out.

What about Nancy Pelosi, the great congresswoman from San Francisco? Where is she on all of this? She doesn't know about the crime spree. What about Dianne Feinstein, the feeble U.S. senator with the Chinese communist spy who drove her around for 20 years?[116]

I say we must track these looting mobs. These mobs are using social media and certain messaging apps to carry out their crimes. And I want to know why Twitter and Facebook aren't reporting their messages. After all, they shadow ban and block my content. They shadow ban and block every conservative in this country. But they don't shadow ban or block these animals who are planning these robberies.

I hope I offend 10 million people by calling them animals. What should I call them? They are fine human beings doing this to our society. They are breaking our society into pieces. It will shatter like the shop windows on Kristallnacht unless they are rounded up and thrown in jail.

Seth Rogen always played a Jewish schmuck. I say this, being Jewish myself. He made his fortune by playing a Jewish schmuck, and he made a fortune, like many Jews did, like Woody Allen. He doesn't understand that now life is imitating art.

Rogan told a robbery victim that Los Angeles is "lovely" and advised him simply not to leave valuable items in his car.[117] That's just life in the big city, according to the schmuck. This is easy for him to say because he has the money to afford a new window.

I had my car broken into not too long ago. I went to San Francisco last year with my family, went to a Chinese restaurant in the Richmond District, came out, and two minutes later I saw that the glass was broken. I said to the Chinese guy, "I've been coming here for 40 years. How did this happen in your neighborhood, the Richmond District?" He said: "Michael, they come by. One is on a bicycle with a walkie-talkie and looks in the car. Then he calls a partner in a car. The partner comes with a crowbar. He breaks in and is gone in a minute. These are organized gangs."

Okay, so let's say they're gangs. As I said, they're fencing the goods. Someone is buying these expensive Hermes handbags. They're not two dollars. They cost upwards of $7,000. So who's buying these fancy goods? You're telling me that the police can't figure this out? The FBI can't figure this out? Somebody is fencing the goods. Why is the cybersecurity division of the California Highway Patrol not tracing the goods? Why are we sweeping this under the rug?

I could go on and on. Did we forget already how many old people were killed at a Christmas parade in Wisconsin?[118] You can thank the prosecutors and judges in Wisconsin who let this guy out for that one. [119] Where are the consequences? Why aren't the judges thrown in jail for doing a thing like that?

Society as we know it is breaking down because of pernicious liberalism. I hate to keep using a word that is so overused that people don't even know what it means anymore. Liberalism is, in fact, a mental disorder. A very wise man published this book in 2015, and it became a very popular book, very popular words. But it wasn't a joke.

In other words, whenever you see something bad going on in society and people say to me, "Michael, did you see what happened?" I say, "Just take what happened and plug this into the formula. When you ask yourself, how did it happen? Just plug this into the question and you have the answer. This does not mean that all liberals are mentally disordered, just about 99 percent of them.

THE SOROS DAs

I've been warning for years about billionaire criminal George Soros's project to appoint left-wing prosecutors in liberal cities.[120] Well, Chesa Boudin, former district attorney in San Francisco, is the poster boy for this effort, and he was so bad even San Francisco liberals recalled him. A March 2022 poll found that 64 percent of Democrats supported kicking him out of office.[121]

So why did they elect him in the first place?

You may have read Washington Irving's classic short story, "Rip Van Winkle." It's the myth about a man who fell asleep after drinking too much in the woods in the Catskill Mountains and woke up 20 years later. His beard was three feet long, and all his friends have been killed in the American Revolution. And he didn't even know the American Revolution had occurred.

Chesa Boudin is like Rip Van Winkle. Even though he was born in 1980, he acts like he fell asleep in the 1960s. The fact of the matter is that the only thing that stops criminals is a nightstick, a gun, and more jails. Boudin is an intergenerational communist operative. You don't have to look any further than his background.

He spent the first part of his life visiting his parents in prison. They were members of the left-wing terrorist group Weather Underground and were locked up after leaving him with a babysitter so that they could participate in an armored car robbery. The robbery was unsuccessful, but two cops and one of the armored truck guards were killed.[122]

Boudin's great-grand uncle, Louis Boudin, was a Marxist theoretician. His grandfather, Leonard Boudin, was an attorney who represented Fidel Castro.[123] His uncle was the left-wing journalist I. F. Stone from the 1960s. The man is an intergenerational hardcore leftist.

Boudin makes the same argument that cops don't stop criminals that we heard from the progressives about ISIS when they were raping and killing their way across the Middle East. The progressives said that we just had to get them jobs. Remember that under Obama? If only the ninth-century maniacs had jobs and were flipping camel burgers, they wouldn't rape and murder. Boudin has the same mentality about criminals here. But he is not alone. The nation is suffering under a reign of terror as a result of George Soros funded "progressive" DAs.

Let me put it in terms of dogs, since the president ditched his old dog for a new one. There are wolfhounds to protect sheep from wolves. So, if you remove the wolfhounds who protect the sheep and then you release more wolves into the flock of sheep, what happens to the sheep? They get killed and eaten.

This is exactly what this lunatic is doing. Not only did the city pass Prop 47 so that animals could run wild in the streets and not be prosecuted, but the first day Boudin took office he eliminated money bail, effectively releasing criminals onto the streets.[124]

He's a communist. He eliminated cash bail and replaced it with a risk-based system. This is why you have these animals breaking into stores. No other reason. Boudin spent a lot of time traveling to degenerate communist Venezuela and served as a translator in the Venezuelan presidential palace during the administration of Hugo Chavez. He's a naked communist.

And this lawyer, this intergenerational communist, is saying that criminals need jobs. These animals don't need jobs. They need jail bars. The only thing that will stop them is more prisons and more cops. That's the only thing. I am so fed up with these retrograde liars on the left.

When even left-wing mayor London Breed announced that the police would take a tougher stance toward the homeless bums in San Francisco's Tenderloin district who *refused help*, Boudin, the intergenerational communist, had this to say: "Arresting people who are addicted to drugs, jailing people who have mental health struggles, putting folks who are selling hot dogs or other food on the streets in cages will not solve these problems, and they are certainly not the only tools available."[125]

Boudin isn't the only example of Soros's legal arson. His contributions to the crime surge include the infamous racist Alvin Bragg, DA in Manhattan, who said that he's going to jail people for nothing but homicides.[126] He probably won't even do that. There is also George Gascón, DA in Los Angeles, who was thrown out of San Francisco. He went down there and destroyed that city. Larry Krasner, DA in Philadelphia, presides over a city where the homicide rate is now astronomical.[127] And don't forget Kim Foxx, Cook County State's Attorney in Chicago.

They were all funded by the same George Soros. I don't understand why Soros, a Hungarian Jewish refugee who escaped the Holocaust, would hate this country so much. Why would he want such mayhem and chaos in cities in America? I can only speculate. How did he make his original fortune? He bet against the British pound. He almost destroyed the currency. He sold it short. Everyone says that it's politics. I say maybe it's not politics. Maybe it's money. Maybe he bet against the U.S. dollar, and he wants it to crash.

Why have Nancy Pelosi and Dianne Feinstein, who live in beautiful homes in Pacific Heights, done nothing to stop this crime surge in San Francisco? What about the fences for all the goods that are being stolen in these high-end robberies? With the smash and grab, that stuff doesn't disappear. It goes through fences. Who's making the money? Does any of that money get kicked upstairs to the politicians? Am I allowed to ask this question?

Every other society on Earth knows what happens. Look, there's a connection between what's going on in the street and what goes on in the stratosphere among those who are supposed to control things.

There is a show on Netflix called *Peaky Blinders*. It's set in England right after World War I, where criminal gangs are taking over. But if you look at the crime in the streets of London at that time, the things that were being done and the money that was being stolen were going upstairs to the politicians, which is why no one stopped them. So the street gangs in England were robbing, pillaging, and murdering, and all the money was flowing upstairs. The politicians were so corrupt that they were taking a piece of the action.

BAILOUTS FOR BUMS

Just when you thought it couldn't get crazier, that Bernie Sanders was as far left as you could ever see on the American political stage, it gets worse. There's the governor of California saying that doctors should be able to prescribe housing like medication as though we owe the bums a 3/2 in the suburbs.[128] Take a filthy, crack-addicted vermin from the street and give him a three-bedroom, two-bath house in the suburbs.

There comes a point when the insanity reaches such a level that the people have to speak out, and I'm going to speak out once again.

I'm going to say once and for all what I think needs to be done with the homeless situation in the United States of America. And that is to reopen existing state-run mental hospitals and build new ones because without civility, there is no civil society.

So that there is no confusion, let me spell it out: Forcibly remove them from the streets, burn their tents, and put them into mental hospitals if they can't take care of themselves. A civil society must take care of them. You don't ask a crazy person what he'd like for breakfast as he is trying to hit you on the head with an ax.

They have what are called "navigation centers" in the city of San Francisco that place homeless bums, drug addicts, and violent criminals hiding in the homeless population in communities with people trying to go to work, make a living, and rent an apartment.

So far-left California has just gotten crazier. California already has 50 percent of all the filthy bums in the whole country. Why do you think California is a magnet for the sickest and most drug-addicted in the nation? Well, it's the predictable result when you put money out. Ants are attracted to honey. If you offer overly generous social services, hand out free needles, and don't arrest psychotic bums in the streets, where do you think they're going to go?

Californians need to wake up and understand that tough love is the only thing that really works with some people.

In the Democrat-controlled state of California, the one-party system has now made California the number one homeless magnet in the country. It not only has the most homeless, but it also has almost twice as many as its nearest competitor, New York.[129] While the rest of the country experienced a combined decrease in homelessness in 2019, there were significant increases in California and Oregon, two of the most psychotically liberal states in the world. Those two states alone "offset those nationwide decreases, causing an overall increase in homelessness," said a Department of Housing and Urban Development (HUD) report.[130]

Now, to me, the word "homeless" is a misnomer. It's an invention of the Marxist left that implies that everyone on Earth is entitled to a home. No, you're not entitled to a home. I'm a believer in the state or federal government taking care of the needy, but not those who purposely destroy their will to live and their ability to take care of themselves. You shoot up drugs and you want me to wipe your behind for you and give you a house? Are you joking?

I'm a former social worker. I've seen what these bums do to the houses they are given. They're driving most of the small businesses out of the city of San Francisco, which, by the way, is what big business in San Francisco wants. They don't want local businesses there. They want to drive the local restaurants and local storekeepers out. The bums are helping them when they go into grocery stores and restaurants and take what they want, and the police can't arrest them because of the weak laws.

The progressives claimed a few years back that the problem was "disinvestment in our social safety net."[131] We didn't disinvest in our social safety nets. We threw hundreds of billions of dollars at them, most of which was stolen by politicians like the Democrats running California. Don't talk about failures in our mental health system. Don't talk about income inequality. That means nothing. Tell that to the guy working three jobs.

Have you ever noticed that you almost never see illegal immigrants living in the gutter? Why? Because they work their hearts out. They have pride. They have self-respect. I don't know when I've last seen a Mexican in the gutter or someone from El Salvador or Guatemala. Most of them work two or three jobs.

The so-called homeless are the leftovers of society. These are the extras on life's stage. These are the people who are wrecking our cities and destroying our will to even go to the city. And it's time somebody stood up to the homeless lobbyists who are front men for the gangsters, making fortunes off the so-called homeless problem. It is time to reopen mental hospitals and build new ones. It is time to take the homeless off the streets, forcibly, if necessary. Remove those disease-infested tent cities because eventually we're going to have the plague recur in this country.

This has already happened in LA, by the way.[132] If you study the history of the Black Plague, you'll understand what happened when the fleas on the rats started to jump off the rats onto people and spread the disease. And then you'll understand what is happening in this country. But it's not going to change until one of these Politburo members is, God forbid, stabbed in the back with a screwdriver or shot in the head like Kate Steinle and then sees the bum walk out laughing from the courtroom. Only when one of the members of the Politburo is affected by these bums directly will you see a change.

But that's unlikely to happen because they live in gated communities. They ride around in bulletproof limousines. They have armed bodyguards while they disarm you.

Then again, of course, there's always all the white racism running around this society. It may have triggered this, or it could have been the Wuhan virus or Black Lives Matter (BLM), for example. But you're not going to hear that BLM is a hate fest that has been going on now for years. No one will even entertain the idea that may trigger lunatics like this either.

So what's the solution? Simple. Install metal detectors on subways. Arrest fare jumpers immediately. No more revolving doors for criminals. No more coddling of BLM, media hate fests, and lies. We have to say it like it is. There is an epidemic of minority crime in New York City and other cities run by Democrats. We've all turned away and pretended we didn't see the bats in the head, the golf clubs, and the old ladies being knocked down.

New York City Mayor Eric Adams was a hope for all of us when he was elected. We were hoping an African American man who had been a New York Police Department captain would know better than to become what he has become. In the beginning, all he did was appear in another $3,000 to $5,000 sport coat every day, thinking it was all a variety show where he was going to become a new hero with perfect clothing for a new movie.

Being mayor is a tough job. It's going to take more than rhetoric to stop the crime spree. And the fact of the matter is that there are reasons why these unhinged people are going off like skyrockets. We have to stop the Democratic Socialists of America, that is, the communist vermin, from attacking the police every time there's an incident like this.

Immediately following a recent shooting, Occasional Cortex's minions said it was the police's fault because they didn't stop this before it happened.[133] These are the people who said, "Defund the police." They want to blame the police, but this never would have happened if the police were empowered to stop and frisk people who look suspicious. I don't care what their race is. I don't care if they look like the man on the moon. There are people who look suspicious who should be stopped, period.

Nobody wants to live in a city or state where liberal policies are actually implemented. Criminals robbing and looting with impunity, homeless bums taking drugs and polluting the streets with feces and refuse to be assisted by designated authorities, and being taxed at the highest rates in the country for the privilege of suffering this hellscape are only a few reasons why liberal cities like San Francisco are seeing their populations flee the city and the state in record numbers.[134]

The danger here is that they are moving to sensibly run red states where they can elect people like Chesa Boudin, George Gascón, and Nancy Pelosi in those places. Red states may need their own walls to protect them from liberals fleeing the dystopias they created.

AMERICA IS AS SICK AS ITS PEOPLE

America is as sick as its people. I observe obesity today to an extent I would never have imagined possible a few decades ago. Obesity, as you well know, is related to diabetes, heart disease, colon cancer, and so on. And you see people eating garbage: ice cream, hot dogs, hamburgers laden with cheese, heavy meals in every restaurant. They follow that up with dessert, like they're children, with big smiles.

Every other ad on Fox News or any other cable news channel is for a medicine for diabetes or other lifestyle-driven medical conditions. "Lower your A1c," they say. Americans seem to be suffering from every disease imaginable. As I watch this, I say to myself that a population that does not care what it puts in its mouth and what effect that may have on its own health certainly cannot even conceptualize a nation-state. It's not real to them.

Just as their bodies are invaded by garbage on a daily basis, so too are our borders, which are busted wide open, being invaded by the flotsam and jetsam of humanity. At least five million illegal aliens are known to have crossed the border under the Biden regime.[135] Those are just the ones the border patrol knows about. What about the unknown? What about the Chinese being found at the border?

Why are they not vetted? They are admitted right into the population just like germs invading the body.

No nation can survive this kind of assault, just as nobody can survive an assault of poisonous toxins, whether it be from food, bacteria, fungi, or viruses. As of 2020, the obesity prevalence in the United States was 41.9 percent overall. Among non-Hispanic blacks, it was 49.9 percent, followed closely by Hispanic adults at 45.6 percent.[136] This is before they were locked in their homes during the COVID pandemic with nothing to do but watch television and eat even more junk food.

What other degenerative diseases are we seeing at epidemic levels in America as a result of the lack of care for their own bodies? I began my radio career talking about a book I could not get published called *Immigrants and Epidemics*. I was canceled in the 1980s for telling the truth, but I was right. Now, polio and tuberculosis are making a comeback in America. Thank you, Joe Biden.

And so, as I say, a population that is sick and does not care for its own health and doesn't care what it's putting into its own body cares less about a thing called a nation, which is too abstract. Therefore, a gangster regime can take it over. Illegal aliens can run wild over the border and in the streets. Progressive lunatic fringe district attorneys put in by the most evil man on the planet, George Soros, can continue to release criminals onto the streets, and the population doesn't care unless they themselves are raped or mugged. The sick, obese bodies of America's population are reflected in the sickness of its body politic.

CHAPTER 8

THE DIVIDE AND CONQUER PLOT

What kind of system is it where it's winner take all? What
kind of system is it where half the country feels vindicated,
but the other half feels like they have no representation.
This leads me to a couple of thoughts and questions.

I TOLD MY LISTENERS ON "The Savage Nation" what was going to happen in the 2020 presidential election. I said, here is the deal: it could well be that at 10 o'clock on election night, Trump is winning in Michigan, he's winning in Pennsylvania, he's winning in Wisconsin, and it gets on television. He says, "Thank you Americans for reelecting me." It's all over. Have a good day.

But then the next day and the day following, all those mail-in ballots get counted. And it turns out that Biden has won those states, at which point Trump says, see, I told you the whole thing was fraudulent. I told you those mail-in ballots were crooked, and we're not going to leave office. So that was a worry that I and a lot of people had.

We heard the naked communist Bernie Sanders telling you that they knew in advance that they would rig the election.[137] How could this old communist have predicted what happened after the election with mail-in ballots unless he knew in advance how he and his cohorts were going to steal the election?

WINNER TAKE ALL?

The preceding leads me to ask if it is time to end our two-party system. I have long thought that this is one of the most broken systems ever invented in the history of the world. It doesn't work, as we saw in 2016 with Trump versus Hillary. It left half the country crazed and angry. And now whoever wins the next election will leave the other half of the country crazed and angry.

What kind of system is it where it's winner take all? What kind of system is it where half the country feels vindicated, but the other half feels like they have no representation. This leads me to a couple of thoughts and questions.

Here is one thought: Make the winner of the presidential election the president and the loser the vice president. In that way, each side has a rep in the White House. This was the original system of government in this country. It was only ditched after the scandal surrounding Vice President Aaron Burr's duel with Alexander Hamilton. I doubt that we have to worry about anything like that today.

So we have a two-party system that has proven itself to be worthless. Our Constitution, as brilliant as it is, and I know many of you glorify the writers of the Constitution as some godly figures, was written when America was inhabited by and controlled by an almost identical group of landowners. Nobody was on welfare. Rioters were imprisoned or hung.

That system doesn't work anymore. We're learning from what is happening right before our eyes today in this country that our election system appears to be fractured. In the last four years, we've seen very clearly that our political system is broken. Now whose fault is that? Democrats? Republicans? Trump? Biden?

FRACTURED AMERICA

You could say that the election of Trump exposed just how fractured our political system really is. His presidency was attacked from both sides because he was an outsider who was not supposed to win. The political system right now is fractured because our society is fractured.

Those two realities are not disconnected. The fractured political system is nothing more than a reflection of our fractured society.

I'm an observer of nature, and the way I get my peace and calm is by observing nature, mainly birds, seabirds. One day, after my show, I went out on my boat, smelled the air, and looked at the birds, particularly pelicans. I love pelicans. They're majestic animals, and what I saw that day was adult pelicans teaching their young how to catch fish.

You see a fully grown pelican, and then you see a chick pelican behind her or behind him. I really don't know if it's the male or female that teaches the young how to fish. You see the tiniest little bird flying next to its parent. And this is nature at its finest after millions of years of evolution. You stare in wonderment at nature. It's restorative to see such beauty, order, and discipline. And this is the only way that our species or any species can survive.

Compare this with the American children we are raising today, many without a mother or a father—no mentor to guide them, to teach them how to fend for themselves. They're not learning how to fish—meaning, they're not learning the value of work or of holding a job. Instead, they take what they want, or they inherit what they need, and they destroy what others have. Remember, many of the rioters that we see come from wealthy homes.

These children were once called "latchkey children" in the suburbs, and they're now being raised not by parents but by TikTok. And don't think that I'm talking only about the poor or minorities. The young well-to-do are part of the societal fracture as well. They may have two parents in the house, but they're left on their own as well, uncared for and unloved because their parents are too involved in their own self-interests.

The mother looks like a hooker looking at herself on Instagram, so the children resort to the same behavior. They resort to drugs or other ways to get attention. Who do you think make up the majority of Antifa? Are these poor minorities from the inner city? No, 99 percent of Antifa members come from the suburbs and look to each other as a family, albeit a violent family that wants to tear down society, destroy buildings, and hurt people. They think that they can do whatever they want. They do not care about any consequences because they've never had to pay any consequences.

In many cases, because of our fractured society, they won't pay *any* consequences. This cannot go on. Like the pelican, like the animal kingdom, we survive through order and passing down discipline and skills through generations. We, as a people, are no longer doing that.

The fractured election system I am referring to is a result of people no longer thinking they have to follow the rules. There is no order. There is no honor. The two-party system is in part to blame. It is set up to guarantee conflict because it guarantees a winner and a loser. We have a system that pits us against each other. And in the meantime, the ruling party, the political oligarchy, can do whatever it wants with impunity while we tear at each other's throats and constantly attack the other side.

We have a ruling class that gets away with breaking laws, taking our hard-earned money, enriching themselves, and imposing rules on us that they themselves do not have to follow. They're laughing literally all the way to the bank.

When the Founders created our system of government, they did it with the idea that individuals would make decisions on their own. But it didn't take too long for the people who compromise the government to believe that their ideas were superior to their friends' ideas. And that's when we got political parties.

Adams and Jefferson, two of the key Founders who crafted the beautiful words of our Declaration of Independence, formed political parties and for a long while hated each other. It was then less than a decade after formation of the government that this fracture in our society began. And now our society may be fractured beyond repair.

CRITICISM FROM FRIENDS AND FOES

Our political and electoral crisis has not gone unnoticed overseas. China's official Xinhua News Agency ran an article titled, "A Hopeless America," in which the writer said that "U.S. democracy is now a joke."[138] At the time, I said, "Holy God, the Chinese communists are writing this, and I agree with every observation."

The United States is now like a third-world nation, and yet this criticism from communist China mirrors broad concern among the American people. It also mirrors broad concern among our allies and rivals as this nation fights with itself, with "unfounded" allegations of a rash of electoral fraud. I'm not so sure that they're unfounded. It looked to me like there's a lot of electoral fraud.

In the wake of our 2020 electoral disaster, South Korea and Japan "questioned the intrinsic value of democracy," whereas Britain's former Foreign Secretary Jeremy Hunt warned about a "potential catastrophe for the worldwide reputation of democracy."[139] Another writer from China said that democracy has not made America great again and that "this is no longer the United States we knew in the past."[140]

It's hard to disagree with any of them. It may seem ironic that the communist Chinese are criticizing our democracy. It is ironic. But are they wrong? I think as an American that they're not so wrong. I can sit here like a knee-jerker and say that the Framers of the

Constitution were gods themselves, but they were not perfect people. There were human. They were humans looking out for their own interests and for the interests of their little developing nation called America. Brilliant they were; gods they were not.

There are brilliant men and women among us today, equal to the Founding Fathers. But we can't sit here and glorify the Founding Fathers until Kingdom come simply because that's now fodder for commercial talk radio. I think it's time to shed our reverence for the musket and the buggy whip and move on to what's actually going on in this nation today.

I know that this is a republic. I read the civics textbook in 1950. I know it's a republic, not an empire. I know all of these things, but the system is failing us. It's pitting us at each other's throats so that the oligarchy can continue to get away with murder. I'm sorry to use such plain English. As vilified as I am by those on the illegitimate left who, through their prejudice, say things about me that are 100 percent false, I am not afraid to tell the truth as I see it.

Would you expect me to say that felons who have done their time should be given the right to vote? No, you wouldn't. Can you name one other so-called conservative in the media cartel who would dare step out of line and say felons should be given the right to vote after they serve their time? No, you cannot. They march in lockstep as they kick all the money up to one location. And they're not to be trusted because everything they say is for self-interest. For me, it's the opposite. I do this for the nation and only for the nation.

DID MOONSHINE MITCH
THROW THE 2022 MIDTERMS?

This is about a nation, not about any man. And I'll continue by saying I supported Trump way back when. He's done so much to electrify the electorate. But I'm a realist. And there's a saying I learned many years ago: Do you want to be right, or do you want to be smart? What I mean by this is, do we want to win an election, or do we want to say we're behind Trump because he did so much for us?

I believe that Ron DeSantis is the future. He is a younger man. This is a very big factor. If he wins, DeSantis could run again. That would give us eight years. If Trump wins, which is highly doubtful, he'd only have four years, and they would harass him from day one.

Now, of course, they'll harass DeSantis as well. I don't think there's much baggage in his background, but that won't stop the Pelosi team from inventing it.

As for the 2022 senatorial elections, I believe that Trump's endorsements didn't help very much. Many of his picks won in the House, but not in the Senate races. And people are saying enough is enough.

People have analyzed the absence of a "red wave" in 2022 from every different angle. But we have to face reality and admit to ourselves that abortion was a key issue. Some people have criticized me for bringing that up and said that's not the reason the Republicans lost. We might want to believe that, but I believe in facing reality.

In addition, there was no messaging. What the hell did the Republicans run on? Did you hear them say anything positive? It was all Hunter, Hunter, Hunter. That's all we heard. Nobody votes for somebody who is that negative. What if instead they had come out with my mantra: Elect us, and we'll restore our borders, language, and culture? I believe that there is a lot of latent support out there for anyone who will deliver that message boldly. Donald Trump did it in 2016, and he won.

Instead, the only messaging from the Republicans was that everything's bad. Everything is going to go to hell. Nancy's corrupt, blah, blah, blah. We all know that's true. But people don't vote *for* a negative. They will vote against a negative but only if the opponent also has something positive to campaign on. Tell them what you're *for*, not just what you're against. And they certainly went off the rails with the Hunter deal.

Hunter Biden may or may not be corrupt, but the fact is, people didn't want to hear it anymore. It was like a bad advertisement. Before the election, I predicted there would be no big red tidal wave on Newsmax. I call the Republicans the pubs. Frankly, they may have thrown the election.

Why do I make such an astonishing statement? Look no further than Mitch McConnell. He was the minority leader. If the Republicans had won the Senate, he would have been voted out. He would no longer be majority leader. There'd be a new leader of the Senate. So think about it from the point of view of the Turkey Gobbler's self-interest and lust for power. McConnell wanted to lose so that he could retain his minority leader position.

People may think that's impossible. But it's not. People will put their own personal interests above all else. People will certainly put themselves above a party and, as we see over and over again, above a nation.

WE ARE THE COMP RIGHT

The debates preceding the election of Kevin McCarthy as Speaker of the House certainly provided quality entertainment, if not an optimal result. It looked like the Ukrainian parliament of several years ago where people got into fistfights on a regular basis.

Most of what we saw was purely about power. People were jockeying for position or positions on committees. But we really need to focus on the Republican Party. What is its message? They said that Kevin McCarthy gave an interesting speech after he was finally nominated. Under pressure from a small group of Freedom Caucus members, he falsely promised to kill the funding for 87,000 new IRS agents and investigate the origins of COVID and the weaponization of government agencies like the FBI.[141]

Of course, I agree with those individual policies, but there is still something missing: a unifying message from the Republican Party. Republicans need to define themselves rather than let the left continue to define them. They need to say borders, language, and culture in one way or another.

Let me make an analogy. We know from high school biology that even a simple cell in a plant or an animal has borders. They are called "cell membranes" in an animal, "cell walls" in a plant. This corrupt Biden gang has literally melted down our cell walls. It has turned us into an amorphous blob rather than a definable organism. There is virtually no nation left when millions are pouring over the border like invading microbes.

If Republicans want to unify their own voters, let alone people in the middle, in order to stay in power, they need to define what they stand for besides opposing the Democrats. They can't allow the left to continue to define the conservative patriot movement. Otherwise, people in the middle will continue to hear nothing but that we are racists, xenophobes, and so on. We are none of those things.

I'm going to give you a slogan that came to me in a dream. I'm a visionary, so call it a vision. After watching the McCarthy speaker debates, I woke up the next morning thinking that we need a new movement and a new identity. The identity is not "alt right." The left tries to define us as alt right to make us sound like Nazis. We cannot let the communists continue to do this.

Instead of the alt right, we should call ourselves the "comp right." The "comp" is short for compassion. I envision a new movement for the nation and the Republican Party. Borders, language, and culture are the unifying themes, but—and this is the most important part—all citizens are welcome. All races are welcome. All sexual orientations are welcome. This is because without the founding principles of the U.S. Constitution, we are all doomed to disappear, both as individuals and as a nation. That Constitution is the codification of our borders, language, and culture.

I first articulated this idea when I created compassionate conservative events in the early 1990s. George Bush stole the name "compassionate conservative" and redefined it. To him, it meant agreeing to more welfare in exchange for support for his misguided military adventures. He won two elections preaching this distorted version of compassionate conservatism. But I coined the phrase and ran huge events promoting the true meaning of compassionate conservatism, which was traditional American values extended to all Americans regardless of race, creed, or sexual orientation.

Again, we must not allow the left to continue to define the conservative patriot movement. We are not the deplorables. We are not white supremacists or any other form of supremacists. All citizens are welcome. And I emphasize the word "citizens."

This is a winning message against the left. Joe Biden has busted our borders wide open. The country is dying as a result, not only from illegal aliens, mostly coming here for the welfare, not the work, but also from the fentanyl crisis and the other drugs pouring over the border. If this is not stopped, we will have the same shootouts in this country between the U.S. military and the cartels in the streets of America that they are having in Mexico right now.

So the border must be sealed, with U.S. troops, if necessary, to ensure that we know who is coming into the country. The purpose of this is to keep out drugs and the criminals who bring them in. It is not to keep out any particular ethnic group. If you are coming here to work hard, build a better life, and assimilate into American culture, you are welcome, no matter what you look like. This is the message of the comp right. That is true compassionate conservatism.

POT LEGALIZATION REFERENDUMS

Besides control of the Senate, there was another issue on the ballot in many states during the 2022 midterms: recreational marijuana. I have a PhD in a field related to medicinal chemistry and have studied these things for many, many years. The first thing I'll say is that the pot people are smoking today is not the pot people smoked in the 1960s and 1970s. I'll provide some facts for people who aren't aware of what I'm saying.

Let's start with tetrahydrocannabinol (THC) levels. That's the active psychoactive ingredient in marijuana. In the 1960s and 1970s, THC levels were less than 2 percent in the marijuana that was smoked. In the 1990s, it had increased to 4 percent. Today, the THC level is as high as 28 percent. For oils and edibles, it can be as high as 95 percent.[142]

People are blowing their brains out with THC, and emergency rooms are seeing huge increases in visits related to cannabis use. A single hospital in San Diego recently reported seeing up to 37 such ER visits per day, the most common symptom being psychosis.[143] Cannabis use also greatly increases the risk of suicide. A recent study published in the *Journal of the American Medical Association* found that cannabis use increases the user's risk of suicide by almost 300 percent.[144]

You have violence that is erupting from this lethal pot. People don't want to accept it, but I'll repeat it over and over. A 50-year study completed in 2016 found a correlation between long-term cannabis use and violent behavior "equivalent to the increased risk of lung cancer from smoking cigarettes over a similar duration (40 years)."[145] And you see this violence epidemic across America. Do not dismiss the connection to marijuana.

Now, having said all of that, I'm being slammed all over social media by the legacy media, by the potheads, and by the pot peddlers, including governments themselves. The latter are trying to cash in on the taxation. But mark my words, the time will come again when marijuana will be not only limited but also likely eliminated.

It's not coming soon because the politicians are not forward thinking. They just follow whoever throws more money at them. I'll conclude with this. For those of you who want to learn more about this in a different format, I did a podcast on the subject called, "Lethal Pot: It's Not Your Mama's Weed with Laura Stack (episode 493).[146]

Let me warn you this is a heart-wrenching interview. My guest was a woman whose son was a straight-A student. She saw him going downhill, becoming hostile to his parents. He was dabbling in THC. It's a dosage issue. It's 80 to 90 percent potency. The kid wound up throwing himself off an eight-story building. His mother wrote a great book on it called, *The Dangerous Truth about Today's Marijuana: Johnny Stack's Life and Death Story.*

Lethal pot is a national disaster right now. And if appeals to their vanity are more effective than appeals to people's reason, there's a thing called "doobie boobies" that is emerging among men. There haven't been enough studies yet to establish the causal relationship, but plastic surgeons who treat men with gynecomastia, commonly called "man boobs," typically advise their patients to stop smoking marijuana immediately.[147]

So, if you're a man concerned about your appearance, you may want to think twice about smoking marijuana. In contrast, if you are a man who wants to identify as a woman and become a female track or basketball star, then smoking pot may be just the thing for you.

CHAPTER 9

THE WAR PLOT

When Trump was in power, we had a man of peace
because he was a businessman who knew that war was
bad for business—unless you were in the war business.

PRESIDENT BIDEN HAS BROUGHT this nation into a wag the dog war with Russia over Ukraine. Just like the popular movie, it is the president's grand distraction from all his failures: the dementia, the runaway inflation, the media fascism, the corrupt education unions, the open southern border. Worse yet, he's becoming more unstable and more dangerous.

We should not rejoice at his floundering and his senile dementia. Anyone who's had a relative, a grandmother, a mother, or a father in an old age home or assisted living has seen this behavior before. It can rip your heart out. But when it is the president of the United States, it is not only heart wrenching but also dangerous.

I could see another war brewing, and it's all "wag the dog" for the media. Clinton used Kosovo to wag the dog. G. W. Bush used Iraq. Obama used Libya. But we're not talking about Bosnia or Iraq here. We're talking about nuclear-armed Russia. If we think that we can treat them the same way we treated Iraq or Libya, we're in for a horrible surprise. We have a responsibility to the human race to at least listen to what they say. We failed to do that before the war broke out.

Their demands were simple and reasonable: Do not let Ukraine join NATO and put missiles on our border. Isn't that equivalent to the Cuban Missile Crisis? It is. A lot of people forget or never knew how the Cuban Missile Crisis got resolved. They only know half the story. They think Kennedy was the big winner there. And it's true, he did force Khrushchev to remove the missiles from Cuba, which was a big win for JFK. But secretly, behind closed doors, the United States had to agree to remove the Jupiter ballistic missiles that had been deployed in Turkey and pointed at the Soviet Union.

This is a repeat of history all over again. Only this time we have an unstable, presenile near-dictator in the White House. This isn't just a Democratic problem. Many Republicans have already lined up with Biden. They're salivating. We've been sending weapons to Ukraine for years, right through the Trump presidency, and Biden keeps announcing another few billion in military aid which we're sending into what is now a hot war zone.[148] So they're making a fortune.

"Beware the military–industrial complex," said departing President Dwight D. Eisenhower. We're watching it unfold right in front of our eyes. This is why you don't hear any opposition from most Republicans. Lindsay Graham wants even more weaponry and more billions for the war machine.

When Trump was in power, we had a man of peace because he was a businessman who knew that war was bad for business—unless you were in the war business. He did everything he could. He brought peace to the Middle East. He decelerated the war with Russia. He stopped the nonsense talk that Hillary had engaged in. We had much more peace on Earth under Trump.

Right now, it looks like we're on the verge of what could become World War III, and why the Republicans are going along with it is very clear—money, money, money. So, the Democrats want war to distract Americans from the fact that their house of cards has fallen down. The American people will always rally behind their commander-in-chief during a time of war and the Democrats have engaged in foreign wars for the past three administrations they have run.

Look back on Franklin D. Roosevelt. His New Deal was a flop; it failed to end the Depression. But Americans supported him once the World War II began. It was the same with Clinton and Bush. The wag-the-dog strategy exploits genuine American patriotism to cover up the failures of ineffective presidents. We can't afford to wag the dog with nuclear-armed Russia.

ENCOURAGING ZELENSKY, DEMONIZING PUTIN

Ukraine is a sovereign nation. But Russia invaded Ukraine for reasons I've explained before without justifying why Putin is doing it. Zelensky is not doing the Ukrainian people any favors. He's grandstanding. He thinks it's a sitcom. He calls himself a hero. The world is now lionizing him. Yet, what he's doing is raining hellfire down on his own people.

Just after the war began, President Zelensky delivered a speech to the European Parliament in defiance of Russia's ongoing invasion.[149] His words were so moving that the English translator could be heard choking up. Okay, great. In the speech, in the midst of rocket attacks against civilian areas in the Ukrainian city of Kharkiv, Zelensky said that this is the price of freedom. We're fighting just for our land and for our freedom. Nobody is going to break us, said Zelensky, the megalomaniac. We are strong. We are Ukrainians.

Zelensky continued to challenge Putin and said that he wants Ukraine to be recognized as an equal member of Europe, really, and he wants to be part of the European Union. He wants to be part of NATO, exactly the opposite of what Putin has said he would accept.

Of course, Zelensky's remarks were met with applause from the assembly of lunatics. What he is doing is hurting his own people. In my opinion, if he cared about his own people, he would have demanded an immediate meeting with the highest-level government official he could get from Russia and work a deal out that is a compromise for Ukraine and a compromise for Russia.

But, of course, many armchair generals on Fox News want full war. The brutality gets worse. They don't seem to understand whom they are dealing with. Rightly or wrongly, Putin considers Ukraine joining NATO to be an existential threat. Meanwhile, in Ukraine, early peace talks were not fruitful because you have a madman called Zelensky who thinks he's in a sitcom playing a hero, encouraged by the U.S. and European governments and media to continue a war that he cannot win.

Actor Steven Seagal called Putin "one of the great living leaders" after Putin annexed Crimea in 2014. But he had something interesting to say early on:

> Most of us have friends and family in Russia and Ukraine. I look at both as one family and really believe it is an outside entity spending huge sums of money on propaganda to provoke the two countries to be at odds with each other. My prayers are that both countries will come to a positive, peaceful resolution where we can live and thrive together in peace.[150]

Seagal has expressed opinions that have managed to outrage just about everyone. Back in 2014, he said that Ukraine was run by fascists and supported Putin. He's also condemned the anti-America grandstanders kneeling during the national anthem at sporting events. He won a PETA Award for preventing the export of baby elephants from Africa to Japan.[151] Whatever else he's said or done, I'd support him on that.

Whatever else you might think about Seagal, his comments underline the fact that this is not a one-sided story. Putin granted Seagal Russian citizenship to try to bring the Ukrainians and Russians together, but this hardcore government, these hard liners under Zelensky, did not improve relations between Russia and Ukraine but destroyed them.

Do you think that this is going to end because Zelensky says we will not bend? And for those of you who think that Zelensky is a hero, I suggest that you get yourself a one-way ticket to Ukraine because you're not coming back. Maybe he'll grant you citizenship. Maybe he'll give you a personal passport that you can show around the streets of Berkeley.

Biden and NATO don't seem to want the war to end. The tank-killing weapons, drones, and artillery that we sent Ukraine are making the situation worse, not better. They're making Russia even angrier. This is like a bear that's out of control. When you bloody that bear, the bear goes totally insane.

I understand that people naturally would ask what the United States and NATO should do instead. There's no good option here. So, the first rule of medicine applies: *Do no harm.* The world is supplying Ukraine with weapons. Do you really believe that it's simply to help the Ukrainians? Or do you think that there's a little money being made on the weapons? I'll let you figure that one out.

I've often said, "Beware the government–media complex." But long before that, Eisenhower warned about the military–industrial complex. The worst is yet to come. There's going to be a confrontation with the West unless the West removes itself from this war.

Biden's sanctions were intended to devalue the ruble, among other things. The ruble did fall initially but recovered to its prewar levels quickly once Putin soft-pegged the ruble to gold. The USD/

RUB price was trading at around 80 rubles to the dollar just before the war. It spiked to as high as 157 rubles/dollar in early March. By early April, it was back below 80 rubles/dollar.[152]

I wonder who is making money on both sides of that trade? If you shorted the ruble in March and went long in April, you certainly made a nice little windfall off this horrible war. Now they're calling for a seizure of the New York City real estate of Russian oligarchs. That's a very dangerous idea because eventually Americans will have their property seized by foreign powers. Be very careful what you wish for.

THE "REGIME CHANGE" UKRAINE NEEDS

The experts are saying that Ukraine has become the front line in a struggle not just between democracies and autocracies but also between maintaining a rules-based system and a system in which the things that countries want are taken by force. Tell me about Canada, all you liberal experts. Tell me about Trudeau, who seized trucks by force. All the left-wing Putin watchers in America have it all wrong. They have it absolutely upside down. They all want regime change in Russia. What would really save Ukraine is regime change in Ukraine—Zelensky taken out of power by his own people.

It's not as if this would be unprecedented. Countries have removed people from leadership in times of war before. Zelensky is no Churchill. He is not Churchill facing Hitler. There's no comparison between Churchill and Zelensky. This man is an actor who thinks he's in a play. The fact of the matter is that he will kill more of his own people than if they removed him from office and put a man or a woman in power who could negotiate with Russia, a settlement that both parties could live with. This is a terrible tragedy for the

Ukrainian people, but it's not going to get better with Zelensky in power. He should be removed immediately by his own people.

I hope you understand that I'm not justifying Putin's invasion. But I'm a realist, and I've studied history. I've studied war. I've studied political science for a very long time. Every effort should be made to reach a peaceful agreement with Russia and end this war. The whole planet depends on it. (Where are all the Warmists on this hot war?)

Senator Marsha Blackburn went along with Zelensky on his idea to remove Russia from the UN Security Council.[153] These Putin haters have no idea what might happen. First of all, the Soviet Union was written into the charter as one of the five permanent (P5) members of the Security Council, meaning that it was given a veto over the council's business. After the fall of the Soviet Union, Russia inherited that veto and was not challenged.

Now, if you scrub Russia out of the Security Council, what will happen? Even our U.S. ambassador has the brains to understand that such a thing is insanity. She said, "Look, Russia is a member of the Security Council. That's in the UN Charter, but we are going to hold Russia accountable for disrespecting the UN Charter, and they have been isolated in many different ways."[154]

The United Nations is there to provide a place for countries to negotiate and settle differences without resorting to war. If you kick Russia off the Security Council, there are fewer opportunities to settle disputes other than war. With Russia still a member of the Security Council, 80 countries joined us in co-sponsoring a resolution condemning Russia's invasion. More than 50 countries joined us at the podium to call out Russia's aggression. This is all good. The fact that Russia is sitting on the Security Council does not mean it is protected from criticism, protected from isolation, and protected from condemnation.

Others with brains also expressed doubt that Russia could realistically be stripped of its UN membership given the fact that Russia can veto many matters of Security Council business. People must think this through. It may make you feel good and allow you to signal your virtue to kick Russia out for its invasion, but the reality is that this might eliminate Russia from the United Nations altogether. This would make it harder to talk to Russia and make it more resentful and ultimately more dangerous.

Meanwhile, Russia sits on the UN Human Rights Council, as do other human rights abusers such as China and Cuba. So, the United Nations is for the most part a useless body. It has done almost no good whatsoever. It's just a cash cow for those who work for it. But if it is not going to be disbanded, it should at least not be used to start a war rather than prevent one.

FOLLOW THE MONEY IN UKRAINE

Many of you think that this war is about the territory of Ukraine, which it is. There's always a territorial imperative in war, but it's always about money as well. Follow the money. Why do you think there's such a fight over Ukraine in the world right now. Well, there are a lot of natural resources at stake. Ukraine has immense untapped natural gas reserves, second only to Norway's. It has huge reserves of iron ore, lithium, and titanium. It is also one of the largest exporters of wheat and corn, much of which goes to Africa.[155]

According to a well-sourced article on Wikipedia, Ukraine in 2019 was:

the 7th largest world producer of iron ore, the world's 8th largest producer of manganese, 6th largest producer of titanium, and 7th largest producer worldwide of graphite. It was the world's 9th largest producer of uranium in 2018. Ukraine supplies about 50% of the world's neon gas and 40% of its krypton, both of which are needed for the production of semiconductors.[156]

The article goes on to say that "it is estimated that over 90% of U.S. semiconductor-grade neon supplies are imported from Ukraine." Could this be one of the reasons the United States is so interested in a country thousands of miles from its borders?

Ukraine was the breadbasket of the Soviet Union and is now often called the "breadbasket of Europe." It's the first in Europe in terms of arable land area. It's a major exporter of corn, wheat, animal and vegetable oils, rye, barley, oats, and other grains. This is a big factor in both NATO's and Russia's interest in Ukraine.

As I said, there is always a territorial imperative in war, and there is always a financial imperative in war. Let's pray that sane people come to the table and peace reigns as soon as possible.

XI TO BIDEN: CLEAN UP YOUR OWN MESS

The disinformation campaign from the Biden gang continues with regard to the Ukraine war. It continues with regard to the video conference that President Biden had with Chairman Xi of China, which is so utterly important. But it's a continuation of this propaganda campaign. Now people say, "Well, it's old news. What does it really say? What's in it? What do I care about it? Has it affected me? I wouldn't have cared one way or the other."

We have a war raging on the cusp of World War III. Eight million Ukrainians driven out of their own nation. And finally, Biden has a video conference with Chairman Xi of China trying to convince him not to work with Russia. We didn't learn what happened in that meeting. It was completely covered up by the Biden administration but worse by the Wolf Blitzers and Jake Tappers in our media.

But I got the information. The meeting between Xi and Biden was a disaster for the United States. That *was* reported by John Hayward on Breitbart. He wrote:

> The White House did not immediately produce a readout of the video call between President Joe Biden and Chinese dictator Xi Jinping on Friday morning, but the Chinese Foreign Ministry produced a detailed account of the call immediately, publishing it within the hour through Chinese state media.[157]

And basically, what Xi told Biden was, "Don't expect any help from China with Ukraine. It's your mess; you clean it up."

There's a great line, a Chinese phrase, that Xi uses all the time: "He who tied the bell to the tiger must take it off." He was telling Biden that China doesn't bear any responsibility for the Russia–Ukraine conflict. That's the United States' and NATO's mess, at least in part. Xi also said, in effect, "Stay out of Taiwan." And Biden assured Xi that the United States does not support Taiwanese independence nor seek conflict with China.

This is a shocker. In other words, Biden threw Taiwan to the wolves.

A SAVAGE REPUBLIC, NOT AN EMPIRE

As everyone knows by now, I'm an antiwar conservative. Not a pacifist, not an apologist for Putin. But I want a Savage Republic, not an empire. We have zero national security interests in Ukraine. To me, this is a clear wag-the-dog scenario created by the failed Biden administration to get everyone's mind off the disaster of his presidency.

We don't want the people of Ukraine to be conquered by Putin. But it's not in our national strategic interest to intervene. Using military force is the last resort. It's for when diplomacy fails. Why would we want the man who left $70 billion worth of equipment on the ground in Afghanistan to now be in charge of the military in a war against the Russians? Where is this going to lead?

This looks to me like a repeat of what happened at the outset of World War I. One major power did one thing. Then the next major power reacted to that, and so forth. The next thing you know, we had World War I.

The only people screaming for war right now are the war profiteers like Mitch McConnell, Lindsay Graham, and the RINOs—and the leftists, of course, who were never peaceful or pacifist. There is also the whole group of RINOs on Fox News who suddenly are war mongers, although most never served in the military themselves. If you ask anyone who has fought in military combat, they don't like war.

President Biden is absolutely incompetent on every level. He's surrounded by sorority girls and frat boys who are third, fourth, and fifth tier in terms of accomplishments. Look at our national security adviser. This guy is way out of his league. All the people involved in this are out of their leagues. They're college types who have gotten where they are through bullying.

You cannot bully Putin. It's the worst mistake one could make. Russia is a thermonuclear power. Biden's people are playing with the lives of hundreds of millions of people if this goes wrong— and it can easily go wrong. We don't have tactical nuclear weapons anymore. Russia does. Does the average Joe out there know what a tactical nuclear weapon can do to a troop formation? Our troops could be annihilated by tactical nuclear weapons.

Carl von Clausewitz was the great diplomat who said that war is basically the last resort of a failed diplomacy. We've got to use diplomacy here. We cannot let a vulgar comedian in Ukraine drag the entire world into war. The Ukrainian people have suffered in the past under the hands of the Russians. Millions were starved to death under Stalin. The bad blood goes back centuries. This is none of America's business, and the Obama and Biden administrations should not have contributed to the reasons why Putin made the decision to invade. There certainly is no good reason to sacrifice American blood in that region. That's my position. You can be a conservative and be antiwar. At least I can be.

This was one of the reasons I wrote *Trump's War* back in 2017. Trump was a man of peace. He's a businessman who knows that war is bad for a business. That's also one of the reasons I backed him in 2015 and 2016. He came on my show a month before the 2016 election, and I asked him, "Would you meet with Vladimir Putin?" He was actually taken aback by my question. And he said yes, he would. He then said he would meet him even before he was inaugurated if he won the presidency.

And we had huge gains for peace in the Middle East. The United States and Russia joined together to destroy ISIS, which was raping its way across the Middle East. After destroying ISIS, Trump secured agreements with four Middle Eastern nations to recognize

Israel's right to exist as a sovereign nation.[158] The previous 12 presidents in office since 1948 combined had managed the same with only two nations.

Peace is the conservative position going all the way back to Thomas Hobbes in 1651. He wrote in his *Leviathan* that the very first law of nature is to seek peace. The progressives are the warmongers. They have been salivating for war for a long time. Hillary wanted war with Russia before Trump came along. Many people have already forgotten her unhinged call for a no-fly zone over Syria while Russia was there at the Syrian government's invitation to fight the terrorists.[159]

Now we have Biden's sorority girls who are sending troops to defend Ukraine's borders while opening our southern border to hordes of third-world uneducated, unskilled, illegal invaders. I have given Biden credit to the extent that it is due on stopping short of war with Russia. He's just that much less insane than Hillary Clinton, as senile as he might be. But sending all these weapons to Ukraine and publicly encouraging the madman Zelensky to continue the hopeless war against Russia are almost as bad. And it is only Putin's reluctance to recognize the acts of the United States and NATO as acts of war that has kept us out of war with Russia. Personally, I don't want the fate of the world hanging on Vladimir Putin's sense of restraint.

The problem is that the people pulling Biden's strings see his mental incompetence. They see the helter-skelter. The people around him do not know what they're doing. They think they're still at the university and can just bully people into submission. And they're finding out that they cannot bully Putin. He's not afraid of these people at all, especially in the context of how he views Ukraine in terms of Russian security and economic well-being. Putin took

Crimea without a shot fired by the Obama administration. Fast forward to 2023, and Putin shows no signs of backing down, regardless of United States support for Ukraine.

CHAPTER 10

THE COMMUNIST PLOT

———

What is missing in this country is the next
great nationalist leader. We need a nationalist who
is not a racist but rather a leader of America as a whole.

———

THE UNITED STATES IS being torn to pieces in an epic battle between the internationalists and the nationalists, which makes the narrative quite simplistic but quite accurate. Right now, this nation is morally destitute. We are told, falsely, that the economy is booming. Many people believe this and so don't care about what is going on. In reality, millions of people are not working, and there is a battle going on among those of us who yearn for a return to a real America and those who would like to overthrow everything and turn it into the kind of socialist nightmare we've seen fail in so many nations around the world.

There are solutions to this. We have the fallacy of international Marxism being promoted by the propagandists in the media and the fallacy of pacifism being promoted by feminists and homosexuals while they themselves are anything but pacifists. They are the most aggressive people I have ever seen. We have the eternal class war that has been going on for ages. And we have a stalemate between the nationalists and the socialists on a national level.

NATIONALISTS VERSUS SOCIALISTS

The left right is now being run by the nightmarish figure of Joe Biden surrounded by some of the most vicious people in American political history who are stripping America of everything but the graves of our war dead. They have not yet gotten around to breaking the crosses off the war memorials, although I saw a bit of that when I was on the board of the Presidio Trust. I saw their faces. I know what they would like to do to the War Memorial Cemetery at the Presidio.

Patriotism and national pride are the only things that can save this country. The fact of the matter is that most people do not understand that the communists and socialists who are disrupting American traditions at virtually every turn have a sinister motive. And it has nothing to do with antiracism or equity or equality. It has to do with a complete destruction of the United States of America. Most people do not understand the mission they are on underneath their rhetoric. I do.

NO SUCH THING AS DEMOCRATIC SOCIALISM

I can't stand the programming on Netflix by and large. It's violent, woke, and has reached a point of producing only tepid productions. But Netflix also brought in a Russian-produced show on Trotsky. It's a drama rather than a documentary. It's a series from Russia in the Russian language with English subtitles. I like all foreign-language programs to be in the foreign language. I'd rather read the subtitles and listen to the performance of the original actors than hear dubbed-in English-speaking actors.

The guy who plays Trotsky is very compelling. After first seeing the show, I tweeted that Bernie Sanders is a classic Trotskyite. People say Marxist. They don't quite understand that he's not. That's Communism 101. No, he's not a Marxist. He's far worse than Karl Marx. He is a Trotskyite. And I recommend you study what that means.

The Trotskyite Sanders has three homes. He calls himself a democratic socialist. There is no such thing. They are communists.

Read the history of the Soviet communist movement. These are all enemies of the people. Men died in Korea and Vietnam to stop communism. Now we have Bernie, the naked Trotskyite who has run for president twice and recently engineered the worst budget in American history. A budget that was so laden with debt that we may never even recover from the interest load. This could only happen in America, the land of the free and home of the brave.

Ask yourself how men like Bernie Sanders, who would have been considered a seditious enemy of the state not that long ago, are now thought leaders among the young and contenders for the presidency. Remember, men died in Vietnam and Korea to stop communism from spreading in those nations. And now we have a naked Trotskyite who might very well have become the Democratic nominee twice if the party machine didn't do to him what it later did to Trump. Stalin also said, "Those who vote decide nothing. Those who count the vote decide everything."

The party didn't want him in the White House, but it likes him out there pushing the Overton Window on communism. And because of the complicit vermin and uneducated adults in the media, people don't even know that is what he is espousing. He's espousing naked communism.

As I said, there is no such thing as democratic socialism. It derives from the Communist Party of Russia. The party had a Social Democrat wing prior to the violent revolution of 1917, after which they claimed it to be the Communist Party. Trotsky was originally a Social Democrat. After the revolution was successful, he was put in charge of the military wing of the Communist Party and oversaw the killing of millions of fellow Russians for being counterrevolutionaries.

This is the true nature of democratic socialism. It's the moderate-sounding packaging for communism. If you listen to the hateful mouth of Occasional Cortex, one of the most racist people I've ever heard speak in Congress, her hatred for white people literally falls off her ruby-colored lips. Then you have the ungrateful Ilhan Omar, who should be deported to Somalia for marrying her brother and conning America with her hatred. We need to bring back the Sedition Act.

JUST ASK MAO

I've been studying Marx, Engels, and Lenin since I was 18 years old. I've read all of them. I've read some of the most obscure Bolsheviks that people could ever imagine. If you go to Google and search "socialism" or "communism," the definitions have been changed so much that college students don't know the difference. They say, "We're not communists, we're just democratic socialists like in Norway or Sweden."

They don't know what they're talking about. I went to the source of all of this because the man I'm talking about was the biggest mass murderer of the last century. It wasn't Hitler. It wasn't Stalin. It was Mao Zedong. And he wrote this little red book, which was very popular in San Francisco in the 1970s. All the cool little commies were walking around carrying a copy.

What did Mao have to say about socialism and communism? He said that they are one in the same. Never mind what Occasional Cortex says, Mao Zedong wrote in his little red book that the Chinese Revolutionary Movement, led by the Communist Party, embraced the two stages of revolution: the democratic and the socialist revolutions. He said that they are different revolutionary processes but lead to the same thing.

He wrote: "The democratic revolution is the necessary preparation for the socialist revolution, and the socialist revolution is the inevitable sequel to the Democratic Revolution. The ultimate aim for which all communists strive is to bring about a socialist and communist society."[160] Mao makes no distinction between democratic socialism and communism. What Mao says is that the first stage is a democratic revolution. Ultimately, though, he wanted a completely communist society. This is what Bernie Sanders is working for. He says "democratic socialism" today because he knows that it is simply a stop on the train ride to communism.

THE COIFFURED COMMIE

I've seen what has happened in science over the last 10 years. I've seen once prestigious medical journals such as the *New England Journal of Medicine* turned into trash left-wing podiums for left-wing agendas such as attacking guns and homelessness as though they are medical problems when they're not medical problems at all. These problems are the result of mental health patients who pose a danger to themselves and others.

LIBERALS, LIBERTARIANS, AND CONSERVATIVES

I've been saying for years that the people who call themselves "liberals" are not liberal at all. They're the crypto-fascists. They preach about tolerance and acceptance and fairness while they brutally silence dissenters, burn down cities, and violently attack anyone who doesn't agree with them. They have no connection with the liberals of 100 years ago, who were more like today's libertarians.

What is a libertarian? What is a progressive? What is a conservative? I'll make it simple. When libertarians drive a truck in a protest, it's a peaceful protest. They just want the government off their backs. No vaccine mandates. That's one issue for them today. Now we contrast that with a modern progressive today driving a truck in a protest. The progressive says not only will I protest, but I'm going to crash the truck into a Nordstrom and steal the jewelry and the clothing. That's what the pickup bed is for.

That's what liberalism has become because it's been taken over by anarchists and Black Lives Matter, dressed as "progressives." There are few classical liberals of any influence. They've all become activists—and rather violent and coercive ones at that.

Ronald Reagan explained libertarianism best. He had a way of making it simple. Less government. Get out of my pocket, get off my back, and let me have more control of my own destiny. This really makes sense. This is what libertarianism is. It is a modern version of classical liberalism, which was a breakaway from churches and monarchy's powerful governments, and it focused on freedom of the individual. This was the *original* liberalism.

So-called progressivism, in contrast, has become somewhat violent and coercive. How did liberals emerge into these characters who are the opposite of what they began as?

This leaves conservatives. Conservatives are seen holding onto traditional values, as opposed to libertarians, who don't necessarily value them as much. But there is a lot of overlap between conservatives and libertarians. Many of us on the right are really a mixture of libertarian and conservative. Both camps want limited government. Conservatives want limited government, but we don't believe in anarchy. This is where libertarianism gets lost. When people start saying no government, that's when it gets crazy.

Liberals were no longer liberal once they emerged from rebelling against churches and monarchies and overtly powerful governments to becoming an overly powerful, coercive force unto themselves. And where this goes is very dangerous. Progressivism is leading to national socialism. Need I remind anyone what Nazism was? National Socialism was Nazism. What Hitler introduced into Germany was National Socialism.

We don't seem too far away from that when you listen to Occasional Cortex. She sounds like a national socialist. Pelosi is a fascist or a national socialist. She only allowed 25 people to attend the State of the Union address. Why does she want to restrict the number of people attending? What is she afraid of?

We have two visions of the future in America. One is the dystopian vision of these communists and fascists. The other is the one generally held by conservatives, libertarians, and classical liberals, if there are any left. They need to put aside their relatively minor philosophical differences and fight the left under the banner of a new nationalism.

THE NEXT NATIONALIST LEADER

What is missing in this country is the next great nationalist leader. We need a nationalist who is not a racist but rather a leader of America as whole. We need a leader who can unite those among us who love this nation and its traditions and defeat those who would like to tear us apart using the fallacy of Marxism and pacifism and turn us into a completely failed socialist nation.

I'm sorry to tell you that the other side is winning. When have you last heard a major figure in this country go on about patriotism and national pride other than Donald Trump and Ron DeSantis? Have you heard one mealy-mouthed Republican in recent months dwell on patriotism and national pride? No, they've all been beaten into a corner. They're afraid of being called racists or anything else that the left can throw at them. And so we are waiting for a new leader to emerge who can unite us in our passions and bring together all the disparate folks on our side who are clamoring for someone to save this nation before it's too late.

We wake up each day and see a weakling for a president who is clearly senile, falling apart, and surrounded by vicious people. He is trying to impose guilt on white people with the fallacy of racism. His accomplices preach the fallacy of pacifism when they are the most aggressive of all. In the face of this darkness, I'm afraid that we are waiting for a leader who has not yet emerged, and I do not see this leader on the horizon.

CHAPTER 11

ADVICE TO
THE NEXT PRESIDENT

THE NEXT PRESIDENTIAL ELECTION will decide what kind of nation we live in for generations. If we reelect Joe Biden or anyone of his orientation, I fear the work the progressives have been doing for more than 100 years will be completed. We will cease to be a constitutional republic in any meaningful sense and take our place as a subsidiary in the global social democracy, run by unelected bureaucrats in Davos or Brussels and administered by multinational corporations with no allegiance to any country or people.

In 2016, we rejected that fate by electing Donald Trump president. I called it "the shot heard 'round the world" in my 2017 number one *New York Times* best seller, *Trump's War*. It truly was a clarion call to everyone who yearns to break free of this crime family that is wrecking our culture, dissolving our borders, and attempting to deprive us of any chance of economic independence.

The Trump presidency had some success, but it was fleeting. This is not a criticism of President Trump. No president can possibly undo all the damage done by the progressive left in four short years. But the next president, whether it's Donald Trump, Ron DeSantis, or someone else representing our platform of borders, language, and culture, can take action that will have a more permanent effect.

I say "whether it's Donald Trump or someone else" not because I do not support Trump. I do. I was interviewing him on my radio show, "The Savage Nation," as early as 2011, when no one else took him seriously. I supported his candidacy in 2016 wholeheartedly, primarily because he ran on a platform of borders, language, and culture that members of his administration admitted was highly influenced by my show. And having met the former president several times, including in the Oval Office and flying with him on Air Force One, I believe that he is sincere in his support for our principles.

I also understand that Father Time catches up with us all and that the ultimate decision of who represents the Republican Party in 2024 will be up to Republican voters. Whomever they select, it must be someone who firmly believes in our principles, or it won't matter if a Republican or Democrat wins the election. If we elect a RINO, it may even be worse than electing a Democrat because there will be less opposition from real Republicans in Congress.

All that said, I have some advice for the next president, based on my life's work analyzing, talking about, and writing about American politics. I use the Savage Republic as an ideal to which to aspire while realizing that perfection is impossible. That is one bit of wisdom that separates us from the left. We understand that man is flawed and therefore everything he undertakes will be flawed. Man has both a spark of the divine within him as well as his base, animal instincts. Recognizing that this nature cannot be changed but can be governed successfully is also at heart of the Savage Republic.

While the left is wrong and, in some cases, evil, it is better at one thing than the right. It is better at winning. The left has been on a century-long winning streak while the right has at best played defense, content to slow down the liberal juggernaut during their brief times in power, only to see the headlong rush to oblivion resume after the next election.

Playing defense is no longer good enough. We must go on offense and strive for radical change, like the left does. Republican

Governor Ron DeSantis of Florida has figured this out. He isn't merely standing in the way of further leftward expansion. He is striking at the root of the problem in the educational system, the corporate world, and the community. The next president must do likewise and sever the jugular of the progressive totalitarian state.

THE CONSTITUTION

Any attempt to restore the freedom we have lost must start with the Constitution. Longtime followers of my commentary and books know that I do not view this document as some holy relic, inspired by God. Those who do, confuse it with the Ten Commandments, which, if everyone followed, would make government unnecessary. The Constitution, in contrast, is a practical document written by flawed but ingenious men. They recognized that it was not perfect themselves, which is why it provides its own means for amendment.

Not all the Founders supported the Constitution in 1787. Most people are familiar with the written work of three of its chief proponents, Alexander Hamilton, James Madison, and John Jay, called *The Federalist Papers*. Far fewer Americans today realize that there were dozens of articles written against the proposed Constitution known by historians as the Anti-Federalist papers."

The Anti-Federalists weren't as organized as their opposition, and their writings were not collected and put together in one volume like the Federalists, but they are available on the web if you care to read them.[161] While they made many specific predictions on the results of ratifying the Constitution, some of which proved accurate and others which did not, their overall concern was the same as that of many of the delegates to the 1787 Constitutional Convention. They were afraid the new federal government would acquire powers well beyond the few delegated to it in the Constitutional itself.

That general concern proved to be prescient. Whether it was the fault of the document itself or simply people's failure to obey its limits is an academic discussion. But the federal government clearly operates outside the limits placed on it by the Constitution. It has absorbed powers that are supposed to reside with the states or the people. And even within the federal government, the executive branch has absorbed powers that are supposed to reside solely with the legislative or judicial branches.

FEDERALISM

Let's start with the powers reserved to the states or the people. You might be surprised to learn that most powers that would affect you personally are supposed to be reserved to the states. Don't take my word for it. Read Article I, Section 8 of the Constitution yourself. All you will find there is a short list of powers that almost exclusively have to do with national defense and diplomacy with other countries. Outside of the military, it allows the federal government to issue patents, coin money and regulate its value, punish counterfeiters, build post or military roads, and regulate commerce with other nations and between the states. That's it.

You may have noticed that I mentioned nothing about healthcare, education, or running retirement programs, which accounts for half of all federal spending. Certainly, it doesn't include telling local school districts what signs they must put on their rest rooms or what they should be teaching their children. That's all supposed to be done at the state or local level.

In 1980, Ronald Reagan ran for president saying that he would eliminate the Department of Education. It was only a year old at the time. That's right. Somehow, the United States managed to become the most powerful nation in the world without a Department of Education for almost all of its history.

Rather than being abolished, the Department of Education has grown exponentially under every president, Republican or Democrat, including Reagan. George W. Bush grew it tremendously with his ill-conceived "No Child Left Behind" program.

Congressman Thomas Massie of Kentucky reintroduced his bill to abolish the Department in February 2023. Here is the entire text of the bill:

The Department of Education shall terminate on Dec. 31, 2023.[162]

My advice to the next president is to leverage his political power to get this bill passed. The sooner red states are in complete charge of educating their children again, the better.

Liberals spent the twentieth century breaking down the limits on the federal government and allowing it to absorb the powers reserved for the states or the people. From 1937 to 1995, the Supreme Court did not find a single federal law unconstitutional.[163] Liberals were so successful that the very idea of federalism was all but forgotten.

That all changed in 2020. I have plenty of criticism for President Trump in terms of how the COVID-19 pandemic was handled, but one thing I am grateful for is Trump's insistence on leaving the decisions on COVID restrictions to the states. Can you imagine living in America today if there were no examples like South Dakota, which never locked down its citizens, or Florida, Texas, Iowa, and other red states whose governors ditched the ineffective restrictions when it was clear they weren't working?

President Trump stood tall under withering criticism for not mandating a "national plan," in other words, imposing a one-size-fits-all "solution" to the pandemic on all 50 states. Had he done so, we would have no control group to compare results. Now, years after the pandemic, we can plainly see that no existential disasters occurred in Florida or South Dakota, whose governors were reelected in landslides because of the way they handled the pandemic. South Dakota Governor Kristi Noem won her 2018 election by 3 percentage points. She won in 2022 by more than 30. Ron DeSantis improved on his razor-thin 2018 with similar numbers.

My advice to the next president is to likewise adhere to the Constitution in any similar crisis. I'll go further to say even stricter adherence to the Constitution may have prevented the entire 2020 nightmare. I'm talking about the trillions in spending under the CARES Act. While President Trump did leave the decision of whether to lock down and for how long to each state, he forced the states that didn't lock down to subsidize those that did. With the benefit of hindsight, I'd argue that without the federal spending, no lockdowns would have ever occurred.

STATE IMMIGRATION ENFORCEMENT

President Trump was also the first president in decades, Republican or Democrat, to make any serious attempt to enforce our immigration laws. And there was some temporary progress while he was in office. The problem is that everything he did during his four years was almost immediately undone by the dementia patient installed in the White House in 2021.

The "remain in Mexico" policy is a perfect example. Here is something Trump put in place that worked, although the number of immigrants affected represents only a small portion of the millions coming into the country. Still, it was a first step in the right direction. Basically, it said that if you come into the United States from Mexico seeking refugee status, you have to remain in Mexico while your case is being adjudicated. If you are granted refugee status, fine, come right in. If not, you could no longer simply melt into the U.S. population and join the tens of millions of other illegal immigrants already here.

Biden immediately tried to end this effective policy precisely because it was effective. A Trump-appointed federal judge tried to stop Biden from discontinuing the policy, but the Supreme Court sent this back to the lower courts to look at again.[164] It was still pending in lower courts as of this writing.[165]

Meanwhile, hundreds of thousands of illegals not affected by this policy pour over our southern border every month. It's obvious Biden will make no effort to stop them, just as his internationalist predecessors, Democrat and Republican alike, made no effort.

In response, some red state governors have finally begun to do something about it. The governors of Texas and Arizona began putting the migrants dumped into their states by the Biden administration onto buses and sending them to New York City. One would think that this should be fine with New York City, which has declared itself a "sanctuary city" for illegal immigrants, and they would be happy to have them. They weren't.

Governor DeSantis of Florida made the most publicized statement when he sent 50 migrants from Venezuela dumped in his state to Martha's Vineyard.[166] Obviously, this was intended to expose the hypocrisy of liberals who claim they care about the plight of illegal immigrants and who also claim they are a net positive to our country. It couldn't have been more successful.

The smug liberals who live there had all sorts of pretty words to say about how much they loved and welcomed them, but actions speak louder than words. And they had those migrants kicked off Martha's Vineyard and relocated to Joint Base Cape Cod, a military base, in less than 48 hours.[167]

It seems the government can remove illegals pretty quickly when it wants to.

There was one aspect of this incident that seems to have escaped notice. It was the words the Martha's Vineyard homeless coordinator, Lisa Belcastro, used when asked what the "challenges" were with the migrants arriving. She said:

> We don't have the services to take care of 50 immigrants, and we certainly don't have housing... We can't house everyone here that lives here and works here.[168]

Now, a lot of people on the right focused on the fact that there is plenty of housing available in Martha's Vineyard off-season. That's a valid point. But think about what she's saying here. If these people are a net positive to our society, why do they need "services" or "housing" at all? She is implicitly acknowledging that migrants are a net cost to American society, a cost liberals want others to pay while they signal their virtue.

Good for DeSantis and other Republican governors for exposing the hypocrisy of the liberals. But we need more than good optics and "owning the libs." We need a practical solution to our illegal immigration problem that is scalable to the millions trying to get in.

Why can't the solution include turning over immigration enforcement to the states? I know what you're thinking. Protecting our borders is something that is undeniably one of the federal government's responsibilities. It certainly is when it comes to defending our borders from invading foreign armies. But what about immigrants?

Go back to what I told you before about Article I, Section 8 of the Constitution. Just as with healthcare, education, and retirement benefits, the Constitution is silent on immigration. It gives the federal government the power to regulate naturalization, which concerns becoming a citizen. But regulating immigration is nowhere to be found.

I'm going to share a little American history with you they didn't teach you in school. Not only is regulating immigration a power theoretically reserved to the states due to the Constitution's silence on the issue; it is a power that *was being exercised by the states* for our country's first full century. Yes, you read that correctly. States regulated immigration until the mid-1870s.

This was a question settled rather early on after the Constitution was ratified. You are probably familiar with the controversy over the Alien and Sedition Acts during the John Adams administration. Most people remember this as a dispute about free speech because the Sedition Act forbade citizens from criticizing the president or several of his cabinet members. Thomas Jefferson and James Madison famously drafted the Kentucky and Virginia Resolutions arguing that states could nullify federal laws that violated the Constitution.[169]

What most people don't remember is their argument against the Alien Act. The Alien Act was passed because French nationals visiting the United States were agitating against the federal government's official position of neutrality in the latest war between Great Britain and France. The French wanted the United States to enter the war on their side and argued that the mutual defense treaty made with King Louis XVI obligated the United States to do so. The United States argued that the treaty was null and void after the French deposed King Louis and established a new, revolutionary government.

It doesn't really matter who was right or wrong on this question. These French immigrants were troublemakers, and Adams and the Federalist Congress wanted to kick them out of the country.

The problem was that Jefferson, Madison, and the rest of their political alliance that would later become the Republican Party (not to be confused with today's Republican Party) were both partial to the French Revolution—to a fault, eventually—and rabid defenders of the limits on federal power. They argued that regulation of immigration was a power not delegated to the federal government and therefore reserved to the states or the people.

James Madison, the man who wrote the text of the Constitution itself, said that the Alien Act "exercises a power no where delegated to the federal government." He couldn't have been clearer. "No where delegated." End of discussion. And what regulation of immigration there was after this was done by the states.

So how did the federal government get involved in regulating immigration? It usurped this power the same way it grabbed the power to regulate abortion, marriage, and a host of other issues reserved to the states or the people—through a Supreme Court decision called *Chy Lung v. Freeman*.[170] The "Freeman" in this case was a California immigration officer being sued by Chinese immigrant Chy Lung for his handling of her immigration into California.

The details of the case aren't that important, other than to note that it was firmly established that regulation of immigration was a state power and one the states were actively exercising at the time. Chy Lung brought her case all the way to the Supreme Court, and the Court, as it has on so many other issues, "discovered" that this power was delegated to the federal government in the Constitution.

Its decision was at least as spurious as *Roe v. Wade*. The justices barely made any attempt to find the delegation of power in the

words of the Constitution. Rather, they argued that the consequences of individual states regulating immigration would be dangerous because a single state angering a foreign power might get the
whole union into a war.

This is a compelling argument for why the federal government
should be delegated the power to regulate immigration, not that
there aren't contrary arguments. But it isn't an argument that the
power *has been* delegated. If it wasn't a power the man who wrote
the Constitution understood was delegated to the federal government in 1798, and it hasn't been delegated by amendment since,
then that power must still reside with the states.

I know that this probably comes as a shock to most conservatives
for several reasons. One, we've held federal regulation of immigration as an article of faith for decades, despite its abject failure. Two,
it has been our custom to live with Supreme Court decisions we
don't like, no matter how spurious, rather than risk violating what
is considered the "supreme law of the land."

I'm not suggesting that we chuck the latter practice and become
Jacobins. I'll leave that to the left. But I am suggesting that we make
this an issue. We have a Supreme Court now that has shown that
it is willing to revisit past decisions and overturn them as they did
Roe v. Wade. There is no reason we can't find a way to bring a case
on immigration. *Chy Lung v. Freeman* would be at least as easy to
overturn as *Roe* if the Court were willing.

As it is, *Chy Lung* and other decisions do leave some room for the
states to be involved in emergencies. I'd say our situation right now
is an emergency. My advice to the next president is to give states the
widest possible latitude, within the letter of the law, in being involved
in regulating immigration. We may even get some help from the left
on this. If it were President Trump or a similarly nationalist president

who made it a policy to allow states more involvement in regulating immigration, the left just might take the bait and bring a lawsuit that could make it to the Supreme Court. That could create the opportunity we need to overturn another bad decision from the past.

I know what you're probably thinking: "Michael, I thought you were a nationalist! Are we not talking about national borders? Why would you allow some states to let in as many illegals as they wish?"

First, yes, I am a nationalist. But you have to understand what I mean by that. I am a nationalist when it comes to any surrender of our sovereignty to international or multinational bodies. As I said, I don't want socialists in Davos or Brussels making rules about how Americans govern themselves.

But I am also a strong advocate for "states' rights," for lack of a better term. I have been for my whole career. Go back and listen to the speech I gave on compassionate conservatism in the 1990s,[171] long before George W. Bush co-opted that slogan and gave it a completely different meaning. I was a staunch defender of the Tenth Amendment then, and I remain one now.

However, my primary reason for suggesting that we give the states a shot at regulating immigration isn't academic or constitutional. It's practical. The federal government has failed completely to keep illegal immigrants out of our country. It's time to stop doing the same thing over and over again and expecting a different result, said to be Einstein's definition of insanity.

We think of regulating immigration as physically stopping people before they cross our border, but that's not really how it happens in real life. Enforcing immigration laws for the most part comes down to going after people who are already inside the country illegally. As with any other law, the government can't really get involved until the law is broken. Before that, we'd be prosecuting the innocent.

So who better to go into the community to find illegal immigrants, federal agents managed out of a distant capital by bureaucrats who don't really care what happens to your local community or local law enforcement answering to your state government? Think about it. The latter know your community and have a vested interest in your state. Do you think liberal bureaucrats in Washington, DC, care about the effects of illegal immigration on local communities in Texas or Florida? Of course not. If anything, they celebrate the harm that comes to those "deplorables."

This is not to denigrate the fine people who comprise the rank and file of our border patrol or ICE divisions. They are not the problem. Their managers are the problem. Those same people could just as soon quit the federal government and go to work for the states. They would then no longer have to follow orders to ship illegal gang and cartel members into the interior of the country to wreak havoc on their fellow Americans.

As true conservatives, we above all value what works over what sounds good or is consistent with some abstract theory. Federal regulation of immigration doesn't work. It hasn't worked for a long time, and it is unlikely to work anytime soon. We must consider allowing the states in which likeminded people live and work to take a shot at doing better. We have nothing to lose. My advice to the next president is to do everything within the limits of the law and the Constitution he or she can to facilitate state involvement in immigration enforcement.

THE REAL FASCISTS

For years I've told my audience on "The Savage Nation" and "The Michael Savage Show" that liberals are the real fascists. It almost goes without saying post-COVID, when we can see with our own eyes that it is the left that is literally working with the secret police—the FBI and other federal agencies—to shut down dissent to the policies and narratives being forced on the American public.

Still, they have the audacity to call us fascists for simply wanting to be left alone to pursue our own interests in peace and safety. The problem is that tens of millions of Americans believe and blindly parrot the propaganda the criminals feed them, even to the point of denying what they can see with their own eyes.

They continue to have success using racism as a bludgeon, shamelessly exploiting a societal problem that was real 50 years ago but has long since been solved. I know this because I was there. I heard Martin Luther King, Jr., speak as a young man and was inspired by his oratory. I was genuinely moved and agreed with his message of judging people by the content of their character rather than the color of their skin.

He would be appalled and sickened by what the new left is saying about white people.

The ironic part of this is that racism was not really an integral part of fascism as Mussolini described it. People tend to blur Hitler's Nazism and its hatred and scapegoating of the Jewish people with fascism, but that was something specific to the Nazis. Mussolini's purer fascism wasn't concerned primarily with racial identity, only unqualified loyalty to the totalitarian state, although he did persecute the Jewish people in Italy at Hitler's insistence. This was more his own personal weakness than a foundational pillar of fascism itself.

"The Fascist conception of the State is all embracing; outside of it no human or spiritual values can exist, much less have value."[172] This is how Mussolini summed up fascism. Now, you tell me, does this sound more like the right or the left in America today? It is not the right that wants to dictate what you say, even what you think, and are not allowed to think. And as for spiritual values, it is the right that considers them personal and beyond the reach of the state, while the left worships the state and its power as a replacement for God himself.

The modern fascist left has also convinced a large portion of the gullible American population that fascism has something to do with capitalism. Yes, the fascists were against communism and didn't want the government to own the means of production. But they were as against capitalism as they were against communism. "Fascism is definitely and absolutely opposed to the doctrines of liberalism, both in the political and the economic sphere. . . . The Fascist State lays claim to rule in the economic field no less than in others,"[173] wrote Mussolini.

Note that when Mussolini used the word "liberal," he didn't mean it the way it is used today. When he was writing in the 1920s and 1930s, "liberal" meant what we generally refer to as "classical liberal" today—generally free markets, protection of private property, and individual liberty. This is what Mussolini said the fascists were opposed to. Does that sound more like the modern American right or left to you?

Mussolini also said that fascism is "opposed to that form of democracy which equates a nation to the majority."[174] The fascists did not want anything decided democratically. They wanted the supreme leader to issue orders directing every part of society on how to live and work. Another way to put this is that they wanted power concentrated in the executive branch of the government, where the supreme leader and his ministers both made and executed the laws.

This is why it wasn't Calvin Coolidge, the Republican who cut government spending dramatically and famously said, "the business of America is business" whom both Mussolini and Hitler praised.

He represented everything they were against. No, the U.S. president they most admired was none other than the left's patron saint, Franklin Delano Roosevelt.[175]

Once you shake off your brainwashing, you can see why. The New Deal largely transferred the legislative power from Congress, to which the Constitution exclusively delegates it, to the Executive Branch. It built the modern administrative state of federal agencies that writes most of the laws in this country. Don't take my word for it. Supreme Court Justice Samuel Alito, writing in dissent to the Court upholding President Biden's vaccine mandate for healthcare workers, wrote, "Today, however, most federal law is not made by Congress. It comes in the form of rules issued by unelected administrators."[176]

Notice that Biden did not go to Congress when attempting to mandate COVID vaccines for employees in general, either. He tried to do so by having OSHA issue a workplace rule. That one was struck down by the Court. As of this writing, the president is attempting to impose nationwide rent control, again not by asking Congress to pass a law but by issuing orders to be carried out by "the Federal Trade Commission, the Consumer Financial Protection Bureau, the Federal Housing Finance Agency, the Department of Housing and Urban Development and the Department of Justice."[177]

For all their melodrama about threats to "our democracy," the last thing the left wants to do is put any of their policies to an honest vote by the people elected to write laws. Why? Because they know they may lose that vote. So, instead, they impose their draconian policies on the public through executive branch agencies acting on the orders of their supreme, demented leader.

This is the essence of fascism, and the mechanism to impose it was built by the left-wing fascist Franklin Roosevelt during the

Great Depression and greatly expanded under Democratic Party rule in the 1960s and 1970s. But it wasn't solely Democratic presidents who participated. Let's not forget that the EPA was created by Republican Richard Nixon and the Department of Health, Education and Welfare—now called the Department of Health and Human Services—was created by Dwight Eisenhower. The latter was the department that imposed the vaccine mandate on every healthcare worker in the United States, following Joe Biden's orders.

Again, the Constitution provides the means to dismantle this fascist system. It says that the legislative power is delegated exclusively to Congress. Until now, Republican presidents have tended to merely order federal agencies to decrease the number or severity of regulations. The problem with this is that when a Republican president leaves office and is replaced by a Democrat, the old rules come back, and even more draconian new ones are written.

My advice to the next president is to take bolder action. There is no reason federal bureaucrats must be allowed to go on legislating unconstitutionally. The next president has the power to order every rule written by an executive branch employee null and void. But since that would cause unnecessary chaos, I suggest a more orderly approach.

Package up all the rules and regulations under each federal department and send them to Congress. Tell them they will have to do the job they were elected for and vote on which regulations they wish to see maintained and which they don't. They can amend some, rewrite some, and get rid of those they believe are unnecessary or harmful. Give them a time limit, after which the regulations will sunset.

This is not a magic bullet. Congress is very capable of passing terrible laws. But at least the people elected to legislate will be legislating, instead of unelected bureaucrats following the orders of a dictatorial president. Subjecting the rules we will have to follow to an adversarial process, where the people voting on the laws can be voted out of office, will naturally make the government less tyrannical. This isn't a theory. Just compare the government when we used to follow the Constitution on legislation with the one we have now. Biden's vaccine mandates would have been dead on arrival.

THE DEEP STATE

Just as domestic law is no longer written by Congress but rather by the administrative state bureaucracy, much of foreign policy is not conducted by the president or his appointed ministers. Instead, a vast foreign policy state has grown up in the executive branch that largely operates on its own. As we've seen over the past two presidencies, its agents are happy to follow the orders of the president when they comply with its antinationalist agenda. When it doesn't, however, it not only does what it wants but defends itself against the president elected to direct it.

Call this apparatus what you will, "national security state" or "deep state." Its agents, especially in the so-called intelligence community and Pentagon, largely pursue their own agenda regardless of the president's wishes. President Trump ran in 2016 on a saner foreign policy of peace through strength. He rebuilt the demoralized military he inherited from Obama but stressed that using it should always be a last resort.

Trump's mistake was to think he could make peace with this internationalist monster. He hired too many neoconservatives who didn't agree with his foreign policy, and they undermined him at every turn. His secretary of defense, James Mattis, came right out and told President Trump he was resigning because "you have a right to have a Secretary of Defense whose views are better aligned with yours."[178]

Mattis resigned in response to Trump's decision to leave Syria once ISIS was defeated. At least he quit, instead of remaining on the job and trying to undermine the president, like so many others. Some of the blame must go to President Trump himself, for appointing these people, however well-intentioned that might have been. Hopefully, he has learned that you cannot make peace or compromise with the deep state. It offers two choices: go along with it or be destroyed.

I am convinced that foreign policy was the chief source of resistance against Trump. There is simply too much money and power connected to the status quo for them to allow anyone to come in and change it. You will notice that the only Republicans who opposed Trump were the neocon warmongers. Liz Cheney, Adam Kinzinger, Mitt Romney—all card-carrying members of the permanent war party.

After Trump's impeachment over the Ukrainian arms affair, I did a little experiment. Do you remember when many Republicans opposed President Obama's intervention in Syria? Well, I started researching where the Republicans who voted to impeach Trump stood on that issue eight years earlier. Every one of them who was in Congress at the time supported Obama.

Had Trump gone along with the "War Party," I believe he would have incurred far less resistance from the Washington establishment. He certainly would not have been opposed by so many Republicans trying to run the world and sending trillions to defense contractors. The Swamp will allow a figurehead president much latitude on other issues.

The problem is that our foreign policy has to change. Being the policeman of the world has bankrupted this country and made it hated throughout the world. Being on a permanent war footing has also turned this once-free country into a veritable police state. More than 200 years ago, James Madison warned us about precisely this. His words were so prescient that I will quote him at length:

> Of all the enemies to public liberty, war is, perhaps, the most to be dreaded, because it comprises and develops the germ of every other. War is the parent of armies; from these proceed debts and taxes; and armies, and debts, and taxes are the known instruments for bringing the many under the domination of the few. In war, too, the discretionary power of the Executive is extended; its influence in dealing out offices, honors, and emoluments is multiplied; and all the means of seducing the minds, are added to those of subduing the force, of the people. The same malignant aspect in republicanism may be traced in the inequality of fortunes, and the opportunities of fraud, growing out of a state of war, and in the degeneracy of manners and of morals, engendered by both. No nation could preserve its freedom in the midst of continual warfare.[179]

I doubt it could be said any better today, after 200 years of additional experience. What part of this warning has not come true? Which evil he predicted are we not suffering under today?

I have always been an antiwar conservative. I don't believe there is another kind. A true conservative always seeks peace, domestically and with the rest of the world. This does not make me a pacifist.

When it is time to fight in self-defense, I am ready to defend the nation to the death. This is why I have opposed turning the military into a social experiment for so many years. It has one purpose and one purpose only: to destroy the enemy's capability to wage war as quickly and efficiently as possible so that peace can be reestablished once again.

This country no longer has a Department of Defense. That's what they call it, but it's really a Department of Offense. We have a vast national security state that seeks to rule the world just as the domestic administrative state seeks to rule our lives.

My advice to the next president is to bring a sledgehammer to the job rather than a scalpel. These lifelong cold warriors must be extracted from their positions. It is not enough to take a few, symbolic scalps. Yes, firing Victoria Nuland would send a message. But messages aren't enough. Fire everyone in the State Department right down to the janitor. Then have the janitor followed for a while to make sure he's not spying for the people you just kicked out. This will do more than send a message. It will cut the legs off the interventionist monster that has wrought havoc all over the world.

You might wonder how the president could conduct the foreign policy he wanted to after taking such drastic action. Let me remind you that presidents conducted foreign policy just fine in the past with one or two people assigned to each country. You don't need 75,000 people to conduct diplomacy with 180 or so countries. You only need that many people when you're up to no good.

The axe needs to swing throughout the so-called intelligence community as well. Make no mistake, the president needs intelligence. To put it plainer, he needs spies. What he doesn't need is intelligence "operations" causing trouble in other countries. The CIA has acted as the State Department's henchmen going all the way back to the

1950s when it overthrew the government of Iran. The chief reason that Iran is ruled by insane eighth-century throwbacks is the U.S. government's constant meddling in their internal affairs.

We are now embroiled in a proxy war with Russia over Ukraine that would never have occurred if the Washington deep state hadn't overthrown Ukraine's democratically elected government and installed its own puppet in his place. This is not to excuse Putin's invasion. But one can recognize that the invasion was unjustified but not unprovoked.

I believe that even after all the interference in that country on Russia's border, war still could have been avoided if President Trump were reelected. The next president must make his first priority to broker a peace deal between Russia and Ukraine. Nothing is more important. Every day that war continues, we sit on the precipice of destroying all of humanity in a nuclear war.

Peace would not be hard to achieve. It may have been achieved already if not for the Biden administration and its coconspirators in Europe not actively dissuading the Ukrainians from negotiating. President Zelensky was elected in 2019 on a peace platform of talking to Putin to resolve the differences between the two countries. And not joining NATO. Whether he sold his country out or has been strongarmed into continuing this war, it is a disaster for the people of Ukraine and a danger to the entire world. There must be peace at the soonest possible moment.

As I said at the beginning of this chapter, we can no longer play defense against the left. So that there is no confusion, here is a summary of my advice to the next president:

• Send a bill to Congress to repeal the 1965 Immigration Act. Make immigration based on merit again.

- Institute strict quotas on *all* immigration, legal and illegal, for five years. Deport all the millions that Biden has invited to invade this nation. It can be done.
- Enforce the Tenth Amendment as President Trump did in leaving COVID restriction decisions to state governors.
- Give states the widest possible latitude within the law to assist in enforcing immigration law.
- Support Thomas Massie's bill to abolish the Department of Education.
- Return the legislative power to Congress by making Congress vote on all existing and future regulations.
- Lift all regulatory sanctions and subsidies on energy production.
- Gut the CDC, NIH, and other totalitarian health bureaucracies and investigate everyone involved in recommending lockdowns, mask mandates, and vaccine mandates. There must be trials.
- Order all federal gun regulations in violation of the Second Amendment rescinded. Return gun regulation to the states.
- Limit the intelligence agencies and State Department. Fire everyone not needed for genuine intelligence and diplomacy.
- Broker a peace deal between Ukraine and Russia at the soonest possible moment.
- Withdraw from NATO.
- Retool the military into a fighting force, not a social program.
- Veto any budget that is not balanced.

My advice to the next president contains the main tenets of the Savage Republic. The theme that unites all aspects of my vision is peace. I seek a society at peace with itself and the rest of the world. This is the foundation of civil society and of Western civilization.

The next president must be as committed to peace as I am if we are to endure as a free country. He or she must be ready to fight with the totalitarian internationalist establishment to keep us from fighting to the death with each other. Peace is patriotic.

EPILOGUE

I HAVE BEEN FIGHTING TO cure our country of its liberal disease for the past 30 years. But I haven't fought alone. Millions of my listeners, "The Savage Nation," have fought with me. We were the Make America Great Again movement even before Donald Trump gave it that name.

This is what brought people to my radio show. It certainly wasn't just to hear me talk. Perhaps some came at first out of curiosity, because the show was growing in popularity. But there's a deeper fabric of unity that binds my audience and me together. We can call it compassion. We can call it conservatism. In the end, it is a desire to save this country. We are at a crisis point, a crossroads. We all know this. This is what has motivated us to find each other when neither the liberals nor the mainstream conservative movement agreed with us.

Now we are the mainstream conservative movement. Let's never forget what we stand for.

NOTES

1   Emily Jacobs. "Pelosi rejects fellow Democrats' 'court-packing' bill,
    will not bring it to vote." *New York Post*, April 15, 2021. Available at:
    https://nypost.com/2021/04/15/pelosi-doesnt-back-democrats-court
    -packing-wont-bring-to-floor/.

2   Betsy McCaughey. "Never mind the cost—just look at the absurd
    things Build Back Better would buy." *New York Post*, October 5, 2021.
    Available at: https://nypost.com/2021/10/05/never-mind-the-cost
    -just-look-at-the-absurd-things-build-back-better-would-buy/.

3   Lee Moran. "Howard Stern warns what he'd do to unvaccinated if
    he were in charge." *HuffPost*, January 21, 2022. Available at: https://
    www.huffpost.com/entry/howard-stern-message-unvaccinated-covid
    _n_61ea6194e4b01440a68a1391.

4   Rich Lowry. "DA Bragg to cross the Rubicon and divide the nation
    by indicting Trump." *New York Post*, March 20, 2023. Available at:
    https://nypost.com/2023/03/20/da-bragg-to-cross-the-rubicon-and
    -divide-the-nation-by-indicting-trump/.

5   Jonathan Turley. "Bragg brings a criminal case back from dead, but
    may have reanimated Trump's chances." *New York Post*, March 19,
    2023. Available at: https://nypost.com/2023/03/19/bragg-brings-a
    -criminal-case-back-from-dead-but-may-have-reanimated-trumps
    -chances/.

6   Central Intelligence Agency. Guide to the analysis of insurgency.
    McLean, VA, 2012. Available at: https://www.hsdl.org/?view&did
    =713599.

7   Werth Nicolas. "Dekulakisation as mass violence." *Sciences Po*, September 23, 2011. Available at: https://www.sciencespo.fr/mass -violence-war-massacre-resistance/en/document/dekulakisation-mass -violence.html.

8   Matthew Gault. "Is the U.S. already in a new civil war?" *Vice*, October 27, 2020. Available at: https://www.vice.com/en/article/qjp48x/is -the-us-already-in-a-new-civil-war.

9   Patrick Reilly. "U.S. sees ammunition shortage amid record firearms purchases: report." *New York Post*, August 1, 2021. Available at: https://nypost.com/2021/08/01/us-sees-ammunition-shortage-amid -record-firearms-purchases-report/.

10 Martin Savidge and Maria Cartaya. "Americans bought guns in record numbers in 2020 during a year of unrest—and the surge is continuing." CNN, March 14, 2021. Available at: https://www.cnn.com/2021/03/ 14/us/us-gun-sales-record/index.html.

11 "Body armor sales to the general public up 600%." Businesswire, September 17, 2020. Available at: https://www.businesswire.com/ news/home/20200917005158/en/Body-Armor-Sales-to-the-General -Public-Up-600.

12 Wilson Wong. "Ex-NFL player Phillip Adams dead by suicide after killing 5 in South Carolina, officials say." NBC News, April 8, 2021. Available at: https://www.nbcnews.com/news/us-news/five-including -doctor-his-two-grandchildren-killed-south-carolina-shooting -n1263411.

13 "Barack Obama's campaign speech." *The Guardian*, February 10, 2007. Available at: https://www.theguardian.com/world/2007/feb/10/ barackobama.

14 "Proclamation 104—Suspending the writ of habeas corpus through- out the United States." The American Presidency Project, n.d. Available at: https://www.presidency.ucsb.edu/documents/ proclamation-104-suspending-the-writ-habeas-corpus -throughout-the-united-states.

15 Martin Maccardax. "Inflation speeds to 40-year high 7.9%, with record gas prices meaning more pain to come." The Street, March 10, 2022. Available at: https://www.msn.com/en-us/money/markets/ inflation-speeds-to-40-year-high-79-with-record-gas-prices-meaning -more-pain-to-come/ar-AAUT4Jg.

16   Sumeet Chatterjee and Meng Meng. "Exclusive: China taking first steps to pay for oil in yuan this year—sources say." Reuters, March 29, 2018. Available at: https://www.reuters.com/article/us-china-oil-yuan -exclusive-idUSKBN1H51FA.

17   Gal Luft. "The anti-dollar awakening could be ruder and sooner than most economists predict." CNBC, August 27, 2018. Available at: https://www.cnbc.com/2018/08/27/the-anti-dollar-awakening-could -be-ruder-and-sooner-than-most-economists-predict.html.

18   Michelle Hackman, Aruna Viswanatha, and Sadie Gurman. "U.S. in talks to pay hundreds of millions to families separated at border." *Wall Street Journal*, October 28, 2021. Available at: https://www.wsj.com/ articles/biden-administration-in-talks-to-pay-hundreds-of-millions -to-immigrant-families-separated-at-border-11635447591.

19   Mary Kay Linge. "Biden angrily defends DOJ plans for $450K migrant separation payouts." *New York Post*, November 6, 2021. Available at: https://nypost.com/2021/11/06/joe-biden-angrily -defends-plans-for-450k-migrant-separation-payouts/.

20   Caroline Downey. "AG Garland directs FBI to investigate alleged 'violent threats' by parents against school officials." *National Review*, October 5, 2021. Available at https://www.nationalreview.com/news/ ag-garland-directs-fbi-to-investigate-alleged-violent-threats-by-parents -against-school-officials/.

21   Jenna Ryu. "Alec Baldwin and the neglected trauma of unintentional killing." *USA Today*, November 5, 2021. Available at: https://www .usatoday.com/story/life/health-wellness/2021/11/05/rust-shooting -alec-baldwin-and-trauma-unintentional-killing/6271260001/.

22   Randall Hill, Phil Stewart, and Jeff Mason. "U.S. fighter jet shoots down suspected Chinese spy balloon." Reuters, February 6, 2023. Available at: https://www.reuters.com/world/us/biden-says-us-is -going-take-care-of-chinese-balloon-2023-02-04/.

23   Michael Savage Twitter Account. Available at: https://twitter.com/ ASavageNation/status/1621904149842653184?s=20&t=zd_y3fjG -Gy1JWlQONjN1w.

24   Betsy Reed. "Iran shoots down US drone." *The Guardian*, December 4, 2011. Available at: https://www.theguardian.com/world/2011/ dec/04/iran-shoots-down-us-drone.

25 Julia Shapero. "Biden says he ordered US military to shoot down Chinese 'spy' balloon 'as soon as possible'." *The Hill*, February 4, 2023. Available at: https://thehill.com/homenews/administration/3844004-biden-says-he-ordered-us-military-to-shoot-down-chinese-spy-balloon-as-soon-as-possible/.

26 Caitlin O'Kane. "Biden picks Dr. Rachel Levine, a transgender woman, as assistant health secretary in historic first." CBS News, January 19, 2021. Available at: https://www.cbsnews.com/news/rachel-levine-assistant-health-secretary-biden/.

27 Pennsylvania Department of Health. "Interim guidance for nursing care facilities during COVID-19." May 12, 2020. Available at: https://sais.health.pa.gov/commonpoc/content/FacilityWeb/attachment.asp?messageid=3872&filename=Interim+NCF+Guidance_20200512.pdf&attachmentnumber=3.

28 Travis Caldwell. "In Biden's Oval Office, Cesar Chavez takes his place among America's heroes." CNN, January 21, 2021. Available at: https://www.cnn.com/2021/01/21/us/cesar-chavez-bust-oval-office-trnd/index.html.

29 Will Worley. "Donald Trump inauguration: Winston Churchill bust returned to Oval Office." *The Independent*, January 21, 2017. Available at: https://www.independent.co.uk/news/world/americas/donald-trump-inauguration-winston-churchill-bust-returned-oval-office-white-house-a7538806.html.

30 Justine Coleman. "Chris Wallace: This was best inaugural address I've ever heard." *The Hill*, January 20, 2021. Available at: https://thehill.com/homenews/media/535043-chris-wallace-this-was-best-inaugural-address-ive-ever-heard.

31 Rachel Maddow. "Transcript: The Rachel Maddow Show, 1/19/2021." MSNBC, January 19, 2021. Available at: https://www.msnbc.com/transcripts/transcript-rachel-maddow-show-1-19-2021-n1255473.

32 "Paris Climate Agreement." The White House, January 20, 2021. Available at: https://www.whitehouse.gov/briefing-room/statements-releases/2021/01/20/paris-climate-agreement/.

33 Katie Pavlich. "Susan Rice is back at the White House with a new mission." Townhall, January 26, 2021. Available at: https://townhall.com/tipsheet/katiepavlich/2021/01/26/susan-rice-is-back-to-advance-equity-n2583729.

34   David Marcus. "By tapping Susan Rice, Biden embraced worst
     corruption of Obama years." *New York Post*, December 10, 2020.
     Available at: https://nypost.com/2020/12/10/by-tapping-susan-rice
     -biden-embraced-worst-corruption-of-obama-years/.

35   "Proclamation on ending discriminatory bans on entry to the United
     States." The White House, January 20, 2021. Available at: https://
     www.whitehouse.gov/briefing-room/presidential-actions/2021/01/20/
     proclamation-ending-discriminatory-bans-on-entry-to-the-united
     -states/.

36   Jeff Seldin. "US creating new unit to tackle domestic terrorism prose-
     cutions." VOA, January 11, 2022. Available at: https://www.voanews
     .com/a/us-creating-new-unit-to-tackle-domestic-terrorism-prosecutions/
     6392482.html.

37   Steve Nelson and Samuel Chamberlain. "ACLU suggests Biden out
     to lunch over $450K migrant separation payouts." *New York Post*,
     November 3, 2021. Available at: https://nypost.com/2021/11/03/
     aclu-suggests-biden-out-to-lunch-over-450k-migrant-payouts/.

38   Jessica M. Vaughan. "ICE document details 36,000 criminal alien
     releases in 2013." Center for Immigration Studies, May 11, 2014.
     Available at: https://cis.org/Report/ICE-Document-Details-36000
     -Criminal-Alien-Releases-2013.

39   Robby Soave. "Museum curator resigns after he is accused of racism
     for saying he would still collect art from white men." *Reason*, July 14,
     2020. Available at: https://reason.com/2020/07/14/gary-garrels
     -san-francisco-museum-modern-art-racism/.

40   Tim Hains. "Biden touts anti-lynching bill: "White families gathered
     to celebrate the spectacle." RealClear Politics, February 17, 2023.
     Available at: https://www.realclearpolitics.com/video/2023/02/17/
     biden_touts_anti-lynching_bill_at_emmet_till_event_white_families
     _gathered_to_celebrate_the_spectacle.html.

41   "2019 Hate crime statistics." FBI.gov. Available at: https://ucr.fbi.gov/
     hate-crime/2019/topic-pages/offenders

42   Ibid.

43   "Quick facts United States." U.S. Census Bureau, n.d. Available at:
     https://www.census.gov/quickfacts/fact/table/US/PST045221.

44   Ibid.

45   Alexander Hall. "Former Black Panther Angela Davis shocked to learn she is descendant of the Mayflower." *New York Post,* February 23, 2023. Available at: https://nypost.com/2023/02/23/former-black -panther-angela-davis-learns-shes-a-descendant-of-the-mayflower/.

46   "And I Still Rise," *Finding Your Roots*, Season 9, Episode 8. Available at: https://www.pbs.org/weta/finding-your-roots/watch/episodes/and -still-i-rise.

47   William J. Wood. "The illegal beginning of American Negro slavery." *ABA Journal*, January 1970, p. 48. Available at: https://books.google. com/books?id=BEd85InqqAIC&pg=PA48#v=onepage&q&f=false.

48   Ibid.

49   Phillip Burnham. "Selling poor Steven." *American Heritage* 44(1), February–March 1993. Available at: https://www.americanheritage .com/selling-poor-steven.

50   Oliver Darcy. "ABC News suspends 'The View' host Whoopi Goldberg." CNN, February 2, 2022. Available at: https://www.cnn.com/2022/02/ 01/media/whoopi-goldberg-the-view-suspended/index.html.

51   Zack Sharf. "Howard Stern says hospitals should ban COVID anti-vaxxers: 'You're going to go home and die." *Variety*, January 19, 2022. Available at: https://variety.com/2022/digital/news/howard -stern-hospitals-ban-unvaccinated-people-1235157846/.

52   Medically reviewed by Timothy J. Legg, PhD, PsyD, written by Jessica Caporuscio, Pharm.D. "Everything you need to know about white fragility." *Medical News Today*, June 12, 2020. Available at: https:// www.medicalnewstoday.com/articles/white-fragility-definition.

53   Norimitsu Onishi. "Will American ideas tear France apart? Some of Its leaders think so." *New York Times*, February 21, 2021. Available at: https://www.nytimes.com/2021/02/09/world/europe/france-threat -american-universities.html.

54   Francis Mulraney. "'Out-of-control woke leftism and cancel culture' from the U.S. is a threat to France because it 'attacks' the nation's heritage and identity, French politicians and intellectuals say." *Daily Mail*, February 9, 2021. Available at: https://www.dailymail.co.uk/news/

article-9242453/Out-control-woke-leftism-cancel-culture-threat -FRANCE-French-politicians-say.html.

55   Agence France-Presse Paris. "New culture war erupts over
     Paris Opera diversity push." *The Guardian*, February 8, 2021.
     Available at: https://www.theguardian.com/music/2021/feb/08/
     paris-opera-to-overhaul-recruitment-practices-in-diversity-push.

56   Stephen Sorace. "Paris Opera director accused of bringing American-
     style 'cancel culture' to France." *New York Post*, February 11, 2021.
     Available at: https://nypost.com/2021/02/11/paris-opera-director
     -accused-of-bringing-american-style-cancel-culture-to-france/.

57   Marmee Rooke. "France: U.S. 'out-of-control woke leftism and cancel
     culture' threatens France's heritage and identity." *The Federalist Papers*,
     February 10, 2021. Available at: https://thefederalistpapers.org/us/
     france-u-s-control-woke-leftism-cancel-culture-threatens-frances
     -heritage-identity#ixzz7OHCLM4bJ.

58   "French politicians: U.S. colleges exporting dangerous cocktail of
     'woke leftism' and 'cancel culture' that threatens our future." CBN
     News, February 12, 2021. Available at: https://www1.cbn.com/
     cbnnews/world/2021/february/french-politicians-u-s-colleges
     -exporting-dangerous-cocktail-of-woke-leftism-and-cancel-culture
     -that-threatens-our-future.

59   Norimitsu Onishi. "Will American ideas tear France apart? Some
     of its leaders think so." *New York Times*, February 21, 2021.
     Available at: https://www.nytimes.com/2021/02/09/world/europe/
     france-threat-american-universities.html.

60   Jack Montgomery. "WATCH: Farage slams Coca-Cola for alleged 'try
     to be less white' staff training." Breitbart, February 21, 2021. Available
     at: https://www.breitbart.com/europe/2021/02/21/watch-farage
     -slams-coca-cola-for-alleged-try-to-be-less-white-staff-training/.

61   Timothy Cama. "Pelosi's message to grads: Be disruptors." *The Hill*,
     May 17, 2014. Available at: https://thehill.com/blogs/blog-briefing
     -room/news/206417-pelosi-tells-grads-be-disruptors.

62   "Zelensky's full speech at Munich security conference." *Kiev
     Independent*, February 19, 2022. Available at: https://kyivindependent.
     com/national/zelenskys-full-speech-at-munich-security-conference/.

63   Jackson Richman. "Top state dept. official tells MSNBC that 'body
     bags' will return to Russia if Putin invades Ukraine." MSN, February
     10, 2022. Available at: https://www.msn.com/en-us/news/world/

top-state-dept-official-tells-msnbc-that-body-bags-will-return-to
-russia-if-putin-invades-ukraine/ar-AATHMAr.

64   Emma Margolin. "'America the Beautiful' ad features gay parents."
     MSNBC, February 3, 2014. Available at: https://www.msnbc.com/
     msnbc/super-bowl-first-ad-features-gay-parents-msna260106.

65   Aubrie Spady and Timothy H. J. Nerozzi. "Judge Jackson dodges crit-
     ical race theory, abortion questions during Senate hearing." Fox News,
     March 24, 2022. Available at: https://www.foxnews.com/politics/
     judge-jackson-responses-senate-hearing.

66   "Ted Cruz asks Ketanji Brown Jackson about critical race theory full
     video." News 19 WLTX You Tube Channel. Available at: https://
     www.youtube.com/watch?v=R9lxFfOgFtM.

67   "WATCH: Sen. Ted Cruz questions Ketanji Brown Jackson on
     sentencing for child pornography cases." PBS News Hour You Tube
     Channel, March 22, 2022. Available at: https://www.youtube.com/
     watch?v=YLEZGsk_g0o.

68   Victor Morton. "Ketanji Brown Jackson says she can't provide defini-
     tion of 'woman': 'I'm not a biologist'." *Washington Times*, March 22,
     2022. Available at: https://www.washingtontimes.com/news/2022/
     mar/22/ketanji-brown-jackson-says-she-cant-provide-defini/.

69   "Nov. 24, 1974 CE: 'Lucy' discovered in Africa." National Geographic
     Society website. Available at: https://www.nationalgeographic.org/
     thisday/nov24/lucy-discovered-africa/.

70   Alex Berg. "World Rugby's transgender ban a 'dangerous precedent,'
     critics say." NBC News, October 27, 2020. Available at: https://
     www.nbcnews.com/feature/nbc-out/world-rugby-s-transgender-ban
     -dangerous-precedent-critics-say-n1244802.

71   Ibid.

72   'IOC framework on fairness, inclusion and non-discrimination on
     the basis of gender identity and sex variations.' International Olympic
     Committee, 2021, p. 2. Available at: https://stillmed.olympics.com/
     media/Documents/News/2021/11/IOC-Framework-Fairness
     -Inclusion-Non-discrimination-2021.pdf?_ga=2.240828235
     .917732256.1650319343-1328524265.1650319342.

73   Ibid.

74 Jeff Cox. "Inflation rises 7% over the past year, highest since 1982." CNBC, January 12, 2022. Available at: https://www.cnbc.com/2022/01/12/cpi-december-2021-.html.

75 Jeff Cox. "Powell sees no interest rate hikes on the horizon as long as inflation stays low." CNBC, January 14, 2021. Available at: https://www.cnbc.com/2021/01/14/powell-sees-no-interest-rate-hikes-on-the-horizon-as-long-as-inflation-stays-low.html.

76 Victor Ordonez. "A bailout or not? Did the federal government bail-out Silicon Valley Bank and Signature Bank?" ABC News, March 15, 2023. Available at: https://abcnews.go.com/Business/bailout-federal-government-bailout-silicon-valley-bank-signature/story?id=97846142.

77 Elizabeth Stanton. "Sharon Stone reveals she lost half her money to "this banking thing." Fox Business, March 17, 2023. Available at: https://www.foxbusiness.com/entertainment/sharon-stone-reveals-lost-half-money-to-banking-thing.

78 Thomas Barrabi. "Kevin O'Leary grilled on why he kept money at SVB if management were 'idiots'." *New York Post*, March 15, 2023. Available at: https://nypost.com/2023/03/15/kevin-oleary-grilled-on-why-he-kept-money-at-svb/.

79 Kristen Altus. "'Shark Tank' star Kevin O'Leary bashes SVB bailout, moves assets out of banks." Yahoo News, March 15, 2023. Available at: https://news.yahoo.com/shark-tank-star-kevin-oleary-110000536.html.

80 Breck Dumas. "Peter Thiel says he had $50M in Silicon Valley Bank when it shut down." Fox Business, March 16, 2023. Available at: https://www.foxbusiness.com/markets/peter-thiel-50m-silicon-valley-bank-shut-down.

81 Ariel Zilber. "Gavin Newsom hails SVB bailout—without disclosing he's a reported client." *New York Post*, March 15, 2023. Available at: https://nypost.com/2023/03/15/silicon-valley-bank-client-gavin-newsom-praised-bailout/.

82 Ryan Morgan. "Fmr. U.S. Sen. Bob Dole now lobbying for Chinese-owned chemical firm." *American Military News*, May 13, 2020. Available at: https://americanmilitarynews.com/2020/05/fmr-us-sen-bob-dole-now-lobbying-for-chinese-owned-chemical-firm/.

83 "Bush threatens veto in ports row." BBC News, February 22, 2006. Available at: http://news.bbc.co.uk/2/hi/americas/4737940.stm.

84 Danielle Weiner-Bronner. "Why dairy farmers across America are dumping their milk." CNN, April 15, 2020. Available at: https://www.cnn.com/2020/04/15/business/milk-dumping-coronavirus/index.html.

85 "U.S. farmers forced to destroy crops with no demand." Reuters, April 16, 2020. Available at: https://news.yahoo.com/u-farmers-forced-destroy-crops-054114098.html.

86 Sophie Kevany. "Millions of farm animals culled as U.S. food supply chain chokes up." *The Guardian*, April 29, 2020. Available at: https://www.theguardian.com/environment/2020/apr/29/millions-of-farm-animals-culled-as-us-food-supply-chain-chokes-up-coronavirus.

87 Ryan McCrimmon. "China is buying up American farms. Washington wants to crack down." Politico, July 19, 2021. Available at: https://www.politico.com/news/2021/07/19/china-buying-us-farms-foreign-purchase-499893.

88 Jonathan Hettinger. "Efforts to restrict foreign ownership of U.S. farmland grow." *Associated Press*, June 9, 2019. Available at: https://apnews.com/article/laws-bills-mn-state-wire-il-state-wire-champaign-e541895e692545ee80d0fc609cf40011.

89 Lisa Baertlein and P. J. Huffstutter. "Missouri legislation may help Chinese Smithfield buy." Reuters, June 10, 2013. Available at: https://www.reuters.com/article/us-shuanghui-smithfield-missouri-idUSBRE95913F20130610.

90 Valerie Richardson. "Texas blackouts, frozen windmills spark green-energy future fears." *Washington Times*, February 16, 2021. Available at: https://www.washingtontimes.com/news/2021/feb/16/texas-blackouts-frozen-windmills-spark-green-energ/.

91 Douglas Main. "Why environmentalists want us to all eat bugs." *Newsweek*, October 9, 2014. Available at: https://www.newsweek.com/why-environmentalists-want-us-all-eat-bugs-276403.

92 "U.S. Transportation Secretary Buttigieg recommends nearly $4.5 billion to move new and expanded public transit services forward and lower financing costs." Federal Transit Administration, March 28, 2022. Available at: https://www.transit.dot.gov/about/news/

us-transportation-secretary-buttigieg-recommends-nearly-45-billion
-move-new-and-expanded.

93   Dionne Searcey and Eric Lipton. "Hunt for the 'blood diamond of
     batteries' impedes green energy push." *New York Times*, November 29,
     2021. Available at: https://www.nytimes.com/2021/11/29/world/
     congo-cobalt-albert-yuma-mulimbi.html.

94   Chester Dawson. "Your Tesla can go zero to 60 in 2.5 seconds but
     can't get AM radio." *Wall Street Journal*, November 6, 2018. Available
     at: https://www.wsj.com/articles/your-tesla-can-go-zero-to-60-in-2-5
     -seconds-but-cant-get-am-radio-1541523098.

95   David Lyons and Linda Trischitta. "What causes Teslas to explode?"
     South Florida Sun Sentinel, May 9, 2018. Available at: https://www
     .sun-sentinel.com/business/fl-bz-tesla-crash-battery-explosions
     -20180509-story.html.

96   Laurie Clark. "How self-driving cars got stuck in the slow lane." *The
     Guardian*, March 27, 2022. Available at: https://www.theguardian.com/
     technology/2022/mar/27/how-self-driving-cars-got-stuck-in-the-slow
     -lane.

97   "Top 5 dangers of self-driving cars." Technology.org, February 26,
     2019. Available at: https://www.technology.org/2019/02/26/top-5
     -dangers-of-self-driving-cars/.

98   Jackie Wattles. "SpaceX Mars rocket prototype explodes during test
     flight." CNN, April 1, 2021. Available at: https://www.cnn.com/
     2021/03/30/tech/spacex-sn11-starship-test-flight-scn/index.html.

99   Catherine Thorbecke. "Biden says he will replace the entire federal
     fleet with electric vehicles." ABC News, January 26, 2021. Available
     at: https://abcnews.go.com/Technology/biden-replace-entire-federal
     -fleet-electric-vehicles/story?id=75488441.

100 Jay Ramey. "Are EV battery plants creating more pollution than EVs
     eliminate?" *Auto Week*, October 23, 2018. Available at: https://
     www.autoweek.com/news/green-cars/a1709966/will-some-gas-and
     -diesel-cars-still-produce-less-pollution-evs/.

101 Jason Hopkins. "Study: Electric vehicles create MORE pollution than
     diesel engines." *The Federalist Papers*, October 16, 2018. Available at:
     https://thefederalistpapers.org/us/study-electric-vehicles-create
     -pollution-diesel-engines#ixzz7OsKHW3nC.

102 "Recycling lithium-ion batteries from electric vehicles." *Nature*, November 6, 2019. Available at: https://www.nature.com/articles/s41586-019-1682-5.

103 Ibid.

104 Kerry Pickett. "Eric Adams called white NYPD officers 'crackers' in 2019 video." *Washington Times*, February 4, 2022. Available at: https://www.washingtontimes.com/news/2022/feb/4/eric-adams-called-white-nypd-officers-crackers-201/.

105 Peter Nickeas. "'The answer is not to defund.' Here's what's in President Biden's increased budget for policing." CNN, March 31, 2022. Available at: https://www.cnn.com/2022/03/31/us/biden-police-budget-increase/index.html.

106 Editorial Board. "Joe Biden's doubletalk on 'defund the police'." *New York Post*, August 9, 2020. Available at: https://nypost.com/2020/08/09/joe-bidens-doubletalk-on-defund-the-police/.

107 Andrew Mark Miller. "Biden repeats debunked Second Amendment cannon claim, says 'no amendment is absolute'." Fox News, February 3, 2022. Available at: https://www.foxnews.com/politics/biden-repeats-debunked-second-amendment-claim-says-no-amendment-absolute.

108 Jon Greenburg. "Joe Biden gets history wrong on the Second Amendment limiting gun ownership." PolitiFact, June 25, 2021. Available at: https://www.politifact.com/factchecks/2021/jun/25/joe-biden/joe-biden-gets-history-wrong-second-amendment-limi/.

109 "Kagan confirmation hearing, day 3, part 2." CSPAN, June 30, 2010. Available at: https://www.c-span.org/video/?294265-3/kagan-confirmation-hearing-day-3-part-2.

110 Emma Colton. "Sacramento mass shooting suspect ordered to be paid thousands by county weeks before shooting." Fox News, April 13, 2022. Available at: https://www.foxnews.com/us/sacramento-mass-shooting-suspect-paid-thousands-county.

111 Sam Stanton. "Exclusives suspect in Sacramento mass shooting was out of prison despite 10-year term." *Sacramento Bee*, April 15, 2022. Available at: https://www.sacbee.com/news/local/crime/article260131840.html#storylink=cpy.

112 Michael Ruiz. "First Sacramento massacre suspect appears in court as investigation continues, more arrests expected." Fox

News, April 5, 2022. Available at: https://www.foxnews.com/us/
sacramento-massacre-suspect-dandrae-martin-court.

113   Topher Gauk-Roger and Raja Razek. "4 arrested in California Home
Depot mass theft." CNN, November 28, 2021. Available at: https://
www.cnn.com/2021/11/27/us/home-depot-california-robbery/index
.html.

114   Steve Almasy, Kyung Lah, and Alberto Moya. "At least 14 people
killed in shooting in San Bernardino; suspect identified." CNN,
December 3, 2015. Available at: https://www.cnn.com/2015/12/02/
us/san-bernardino-shooting/index.html.

115   "Full text of Apple CEO Tim Cook's open letter on FBI court ruling."
NBC News, February 17, 2016. Available at: https://www.nbcnews
.com/storyline/san-bernardino-shooting/full-text-apple-ceo-tim-cook
-s-open-letter-fbi-n519886.

116   Ethan Epstein. "The spy who drove her: Dianne Feinstein and
Chinese espionage." *Washington Examiner*, September 10, 2018.
Available at: https://www.washingtonexaminer.com/weekly-standard/
the-spy-who-drove-her-dianne-feinstein-and-chinese-espionage.

117   Joshua Rhett Miller. "Seth Rogen ripped for downplaying crime in
Los Angeles as life in 'big city'." *New York Post*, November 26, 2021.
Available at: https://nypost.com/2021/11/26/seth-rogen-roasted-for
-downplaying-crime-in-los-angeles-as-life-in-big-city/.

118   Travis Caldwell, Joe Sutton, Keith Allen, and Kelly McCleary. "What
we know about what happened at the Wisconsin Christmas parade."
CNN, November 22, 2021. Available at: https://www.cnn.com/
2021/11/22/us/wisconsin-christmas-parade-suv-into-crowd-what-we
-know/index.html.

119   Brendan O'Brien and Cheney Orr. "Suspect in Wisconsin parade
carnage was out on bail from previous case." Reuters, November 23,
2021. Available at: https://www.reuters.com/world/us/five-dead
-dozens-injured-after-suv-plows-into-wisconsin-christmas-parade
-2021-11-22/.

120   Isabel Vincent. "How George Soros funded progressive 'legal arsonist'
DAs behind U.S. crime surge." *New York Post*, December 16, 2021.
Available at: https://nypost.com/2021/12/16/how-george-soros
-funded-progressive-das-behind-us-crime-surge/.

121   Heather Knight. "DA Chesa Boudin recall: New poll of S.F. voters suggests he might be in trouble." *San Francisco Chronicle*, March 16, 2022. Available at: https://www.msn.com/en-us/news/us/d-a-chesa -boudin-recall-new-poll-of-s-f-voters-suggests-he-might-be-in-trouble/ ar-AAV7JZm.

122   Allan Smith. "Parents guilty of murder and raised by radicals, Chesa Boudin is San Francisco's next district attorney." NBC News, December 16, 2019. Available at: https://www.nbcnews.com/politics/ elections/parents-guilty-murder-raised-radicals-chesa-boudin-san -francisco-s-n1101071.

123   Lee Stranahan. "The gory details about terrorist teacher Kathy Boudin." Breitbart, April 4, 2013. Available at: https://www.breitbart.com/ politics/2013/04/04the-gory-details-about-terrorist-teacher-kathy -boudin/.

124   Colin Doyle. "Chesa Boudin's new bail policy is nation's most progres- sive. It also reveals persistence of tough-on-crime norms." The Appeal, January 30, 2020. Available at: https://theappeal.org/politicalreport/ chesa-boudin-cash-bail-predictions/.

125   Monique Beals. "San Francisco officials push back on mayor's plan for troubled neighborhood." *The Hill*, December 21, 2021. Available at: https://thehill.com/homenews/state-watch/586716-san-francisco -officials-push-back-on-mayors-plan-to-crack-down-on-crime/.

126   Larry Celona, Tamar Lapin, Tina Moore, Reuven Fenton, and Bruce Golding. "Manhattan DA to stop seeking prison sentences in slew of criminal cases." *New York Post*, January 4, 2022. Available at: https:// nypost.com/2022/01/04/manhattan-da-alvin-bragg-to-stop-seeking -prison-in-some-cases/.

127   Madeleine Wright. "Philadelphia reaches 100th homicide of 2022, on pace to surpass last year's record." 3 CBS Philly, March 11, 2022. Available at: https://philadelphia.cbslocal.com/2022/03/11/ philadelphia-100-homicides-on-pace-record-gun-violence/.

128   Madison Dibble. "California governor: 'Doctors should be able to write prescriptions for housing'." *Washington Examiner*, February 21, 2020. Available at: https://www.washingtonexaminer.com/news/ california-governor-doctors-should-be-able-to-write-prescriptions-for -housing.

129 "Homelessness statistics by state." United States Interagency Council on Homeless, n.d. Available at: https://www.usich.gov/tools-for -action/map/#fn[]=1300&fn[]=2900&fn[]=6400&fn[]=10200&fn[] =13400.

130 Alexa Mae Asperin. "Feds blame California, Oregon for national rise in homelessness." KRON San Francisco, January 2, 2020. Available at: https://www.kron4.com/news/california/feds-blame-california-oregon -for-national-rise-in-homelessness/.

131 Nick Cahill. "Newsom calls homeless crisis 'a disgrace,'" vows change for California." Courthouse News Service, February 19, 2020. Available at: https://www.courthousenews.com/newsom-calls -homeless-crisis-a-disgrace-vows-change-for-california/.

132 Matt Vespa. "Bubonic plague in Los Angeles? Is California on the verge of becoming a third-world state?" Townhall, June 25, 2019. Available at: https://townhall.com/tipsheet/mattvespa/2019/06/25/ bubonic-plague-in-los-angeles-is-california-on-the-verge-of-becoming -our-first-thirdworld-state-n2548969.

133 Emma Colton. "Defund NYPD group says police 'failed' after subway attack, offer 'holistic' alternative" Fox News, April 14, 2022. Available at: https://www.foxnews.com/us/democratic-socialists-of-america -eric-adams-bloated-nypd-presence-subway.

134 Theodore Bunker. "Los Angeles, San Francisco see notable population declines." Newsmax, March 25, 2022. Available at: https:// www.newsmax.com/us/san-francisco-california-los-angeles -population/2022/03/25/id/1062951/.

135 "CBP enforcement statistics fiscal year 2023." U.S. Customs and Border Protection website, 2024. Available at: https://www.cbp.gov/ newsroom/stats/cbp-enforcement-statistics.

136 "Adult obesity facts." Centers for Disease Control and Prevention website, n.d. Available at: https://www.cdc.gov/obesity/data/adult .html.

137 Dawson White. "Here's what Bernie Sanders said in October would happen election night—and it did." *Miami Herald*, November 4, 2020. Available at: https://www.miamiherald.com/news/politics -government/election/article246959347.html.

138 Gerry Shih (*Washington Post*). "China is awash with schadenfreude over U.S. election tumult." SFGate, November 5, 2020. Available

at: https://www.sfgate.com/news/article/China-is-awash-with
-schadenfreude-over-U-S-15703538.php.

139   Ibid.

140   Ibid

141   Jon Levine and Mary Kay Linge. "Freedom Caucus earns major
concessions from Kevin McCarthy after speaker vote." *New York
Post*, January 7, 2023. Available at: https://nypost.com/2023/01/07/
freedom-caucus-earns-major-concessions-from-kevin-mccarthy/.

142   Elizabeth Stuyt. "The problem with the current high potency THC
marijuana from the perspective of an addiction psychiatrist." *Journal
of the Missouri State Medical Association*, November–December
2018. Available at: https://www.ncbi.nlm.nih.gov/pmc/articles/
PMC6312155/.

143   Leighton Woodhouse. "San Diego ERs seeing up to 37 marijuana
cases a day—mostly psychosis." *New York Post*, October 22, 2022.
Available at: https://nypost.com/2022/10/22/san-diego-er-seeing-up
-to-37-marijuana-cases-a-day/.

144   Cynthia A. Fontanella, Danielle L. Steelesmith, Guy Brock, et al.
"Association of cannabis use with self-harm and mortality risk among
youths with mood disorders." *JAMA Pediatrics*, January 19, 2021.
Available at: https://jamanetwork.com/journals/jamapediatrics/
fullarticle/2775255.

145   R. Douglas Fields. "Marijuana use may increase violent behavior."
Psychology Today, March 20, 2016. Available at: https://www
.psychologytoday.com/us/blog/the-new-brain/201603/marijuana
-use-may-increase-violent-behavior.

146   Michael Savage. "Lethal pot: It's not your mama's weed with Laura
Stack (episode 493)." The Michael Savage Show. Available at:
https://michaelsavage.com/lethal-pot-its-not-your-mamas-weed-with
-laura-stack-episode-493/.

147   Anthony Youn. "Does smoking pot cause man boobs?" CNN,
December 5, 2013. Available at: https://www.cnn.com/2013/12/05/
health/youn-pot-moobs/index.html.

148   Joe Gould and Meghann Myers. "U.S. unveils $800 million in weap-
ons and equipment, plus training, for Ukraine." Yahoo News, April
13, 2022. Available at: https://news.yahoo.com/us-unveils-800
-million-weapons-211110393.html.

149 Elisha Fieldstadt. "Zelenskyy gets standing ovation after speech to European Parliament: 'Nobody is going to break us'." NBC News, March 1, 2022. Available at: https://www.nbcnews.com/news/world/ zelenskyy-gets-standing-ovation-speech-european-parliament-rcna18179.

150 Patrick Reilly. "Putin pal Steven Seagal speaks out on Ukraine invasion: 'I look at both as one family'." *New York Post*, February 28, 2022. Available at: https://nypost.com/2022/02/28/putin-pal-steven -seagal-speaks-out-on-ukraine-invasion-i-look-at-both-as-one-family/.

151 Emily Lodish. "Steven Seagal: International man of mystery." GlobalPost, June 7, 2013. Available at: https://theworld.org/dispatch/ news/culture-lifestyle/entertainment/130606/steven-seagal-russia-arms -trade.

152 USD/Rubles. Tradingview.com. Available at: https://www.tradingview .com/chart/?symbol=FX_IDC%3AUSDRUB.

153 Peter Hasson. "Republicans introduce joint resolution demanding Russia lose permanent seat on UN Security Council." Fox News, February 28, 2022. Available at: https://www.foxnews.com/politics/ republicans-introduce-joint-resolution-demanding-russia-lose-veto -power-at-un-security-council.

154 Melanie Arter. "UN Ambassador: 'We are going to hold Russia accountable for disrespecting the UN Charter'." CNS News, February 28, 2022. Available at: https://cnsnews.com/index.php/article/ washington/melanie-arter/un-ambassador-we-are-going-hold-russia -accountable-disrespecting.

155 "Are Ukraine's vast natural resources a real reason behind Russia's invasion?" *Business Today*, February 24, 2022. Available at: https:// www.businesstoday.in/latest/world/story/are-ukraines-vast-natural -resources-a-real-reason-behind-russias-invasion-323894-2022-02-25.

156 "Economy of Ukraine." Wikipedia. Available at: https://en.wikipedia .org/wiki/Economy_of_Ukraine.

157 John Hayward. "China: Xi Jinping tells Biden to clean up his own mess in Ukraine." Breitbart, March 18, 2022. Available at: https://www.breitbart.com/national-security/2022/03/18/ china-xi-jinping-tells-biden-clean-up-his-own-mess-ukraine/.

158 Michael Goodwin. "Middle East peace deals were Trump's mission impossible made possible: Goodwin." *New York Post*, December 29,

2020. Available at: https://nypost.com/2020/12/29/middle-east-peace
-deals-were-trumps-mission-possible-goodwin/.

159   Alex Seitz-Wald. "Hillary Clinton calls for no-fly zone in Syria."
MSNBC, October 1, 2015. Available at: https://www.msnbc.com/
msnbc/hillary-clinton-calls-no-fly-zones-syria-msna694641.

160   Mao Zedong. Quotations from Mao Tse-Tung. CMG Archives, 1966,
p. 10. Available at: https://campbellmgold.co.uk/archive_definitive/
red_book_chairman_mao_1966.pdf.

161   "The AntiFederalist Papers." Internet Archive, n.d. Available at:
https://ia801404.us.archive.org/3/items/TheAntiFederalistPapers/
TheAntiFederalistPapers.pdf.

162   Michael W. Chapman. "Rep. Massie re-introduces bill to abolish
Department of Education." CNS News, February 16, 2023. Available
at: https://www.cnsnews.com/article/washington/michael-w-chapman/
rep-massie-re-introduces-bill-abolish-department-education.

163   "Commerce clause." Cornell School of Law, July 2022. Available at:
https://www.law.cornell.edu/wex/commerce_clause.

164   *Biden et al. v. Texas et al. Supreme Court of the United States*, June 30,
2022. Available at: https://www.supremecourt.gov/opinions/21pdf/
21-954_7l48.pdf.

165   Associated Press. "Judge blocks Biden bid to end 'Remain in Mexico'
policy." PBS, December 16, 2022. Available at: https://www.pbs.org/
newshour/amp/politics/us-judge-blocks-biden-bid-to-end-remain-in
-mexico-policy.

166   Associated Press. "DeSantis flies two planes of migrants to Martha's
Vineyard." NBC News, September 15, 2022. Available at: https://
www.nbcnews.com/news/us-news/desantis-flies-two-planes
-migrants-marthas-vineyard-rcna47841.

167   Jaclyn Diaz. "Migrants sent to Martha's Vineyard are being rehoused
on a base in Cape Cod." NPR, September 16, 2022. Available at:
https://www.npr.org/2022/09/16/1123521033/marthas-vineyard
-migrants-sent-to-cape-cod.

168   Louis Casiano. "Martha's Vineyard homeless advocate says migrants
there will eventually have to move 'somewhere else'." Fox News,
September 15, 2022. Available at: https://www.foxnews.com/us/
marthas-vineyard-homeless-advocate-says-migrants-eventually-have
-move-somewhere.

169 "Virginia and Kentucky Resolutions (1798)." Bill of Rights Institute, n.d. Available at: https://billofrightsinstitute.org/primary-sources/virginia-and-kentucky-resolutions.

170 *Chy Lung v. Freeman, 92 U.S. 275* (1875). Justia, n.d. Available at: https://supreme.justia.com/cases/federal/us/92/275/.

171 "Should we be compassionate conservatives?" The Michael Savage Show (Episode 509), January 10, 2023. Available at: https://podcasts.apple.com/us/podcast/the-michael-savage-show/id635045292?i=1000593415524.

172 "The doctrine of Fascism, Benito Mussolini (1932)." World Future Fund, n.d. Available at: http://www.worldfuturefund.org/wffmaster/Reading/Germany/mussolini.htm.

173 Ibid.

174 Ibid.

175 David Gordon. "Three new deals: Why the Nazis and Fascists loved FDR." Mises Institute, September 13, 2018. Available at: https://mises.org/library/three-new-deals-why-nazis-and-fascists-loved-fdr.

176 Justice Samuel Alito. Dissenting, *Biden v. Missouri*. Cornell Law School website, n.d. Available at: https://www.law.cornell.edu/supremecourt/text/21A240.

177 Anna Bahney. "Biden administration unveils renter protections." CNN, January 25, 2023. Available at: https://www.cnn.com/2023/01/25/homes/biden-tenant-protection-renters/index.html.

178 James Mattis. "Letter of resignation." Department of Defense, December 20, 2018. Available at: https://media.defense.gov/2018/dec/20/2002075156/-1/-1/1/letter-from-secretary-james-n-mattis.pdf.

179 James Madison. *Political Observations*, April 20, 1795. Available at: https://founders.archives.gov/documents/Madison/01-15-02-0423.

ACKNOWLEDGMENT

The author thanks Tom Mullen, who helped to shape this book.

ABOUT THE AUTHOR

DR. MICHAEL SAVAGE is a multimedia icon in the conservative movement, heard by 10 million listeners a week on "The Savage Nation." In 2019, he launched The Savage Nation Podcast with one of the most successful podcast debuts. He is also the author of more than 25 books, including nine *New York Times* best sellers. In 2007, his media presence and profile earned him the coveted Freedom of Speech Award from *Talkers Magazine*.

Michael's passion to unearth the truth about liberalism, borders, language, and culture and his unparalleled stand for America's families have made him the most important figure in the fight for free speech and ideals in America today.

Michael is the only member of the U.S. media ever blacklisted and banned from a Western nation. His ban from visiting Britain in June 2009 has made him the "poster child" for free speech not only for Americans concerned about the cultural shift toward totalitarianism and their right to freedom of expression but also for people around the globe. In mid-2009, the worldwide media attention concerning the ban resulted in a *New Yorker* magazine profile of him.

Michael's illustrious career reached a capstone in 2016 with his induction into the National Radio Hall of Fame. In a break from tradition, listeners were called on to vote on the nominees. Radio listeners overwhelmingly selected Savage over a number of high-profile contenders. Savage also was instrumental in the populist movement that catapulted Donald Trump to the White House in the 2016 presidential election.

Dr. Savage holds a master's degree in medical botany and a second in medical anthropology. Additionally, he earned his PhD from the University of California at Berkeley in epidemiology and nutrition sciences. He is an ardent conservationist, is dedicated to his family, and is a proud patriot of his country.